# THE
# *Aunt Daisy*
## BAKING BOOK

Hodder Moa

*Thank you to The Vintage Table and all others*
*who supplied crockery and cutlery for the photographs*

National Library of New Zealand Cataloguing-in-Publication Data
Daisy, Aunt, 1879-1963.
The Aunt Daisy baking book / Maud "Aunt Daisy" Basham ; Barbara Basham.
ISBN 978-1-86971-227-3
1. Baking.
I. Basham, Barbara. II. Title.
641.815—dc 22

A Hodder Moa Book
Published in 2011 by Hachette New Zealand Ltd
4 Whetu Place, Mairangi Bay
Auckland, New Zealand
www.hachette.co.nz

Photographs by Simon Young
Food styling by Pippa Cuthbert
Designed and produced by Hachette New Zealand Ltd
Printed by Everbest Printing Co Ltd

# Contents

# Foreword

This heritage collection of well-loved, tried and true Aunt Daisy recipes was originally read over ZB radio to housewives, mothers and cooks all over New Zealand from the 1930s to the 1960s.

Armed with pen and paper, many of our grandparents waited eagerly by the wireless to scribble down the latest great recipe for a succulent roast meal, a really good pavlova, or a moist golden syrup pudding to impress their families and friends. They knew that, with Aunt Daisy testing every recipe, they could be counted on to work.

It was a different time and, many will argue, a different world, but this is the kind of food most of us love to remember. It's comfort food in the best sense.

Aunt Daisy's late daughter Barbara Basham researched and compiled *The Aunt Daisy Cookbook* (from which these recipes are taken) as a tribute to her mother. Before Barbara died, she arranged to establish a charitable trust under her Will to which all sale proceeds from this book will go.

The Barbara Basham Medical Charitable Trust is managed by Guardian Trust to fund world-class medical research in New Zealand. The Trust has already enabled the completion of ground-breaking stroke research on improving treatment outcomes.

If you would like to support the Barbara Basham Medical Charitable Trust in this aim, donations are tax-deductible and can be made at any branch of Guardian Trust, or by cheque (payable to the Barbara Basham Medical Charitable Trust) to PO Box 1934, Auckland.

We hope you and your family enjoy these recipes that little bit more, knowing that the sale proceeds of this collection will fund ongoing medical research in New Zealand.

*Guardian Trust*

# About The Aunt Daisy Baking Book

Recipes in *The Aunt Daisy Baking Book* come from *The Aunt Daisy Cookbook*, which is one of New Zealand's bestselling recipe books. It was first published in 1968. Although Aunt Daisy's recipes themselves stand the test of time, some measurements and methods have changed over the years.

Aunt Daisy's recipes often presumed the cook had a good amount of know-how, and so give instructions such as 'cook as usual' or 'bake in the usual way'. In the recipes that were particularly sparse and where today's cooks would have difficulty, some extra instructions have been added to clarify.

## Ingredients

There are no unusual or uncommon ingredients in these recipes. In the 'Breads, Scones & Teacakes' section of this book, Aunt Daisy's recipes call for 'compressed yeast'. Compressed yeast is still available but active dry yeast is more common these days. To convert, active dry yeast can be used at 50 per cent of the weight of fresh compressed yeast.

## Measurements

All recipes have been metricated. Pounds and ounces have been changed to grams, quarts and pints to millilitres, and inches to centimetres.

Breakfast cup and teacup measures remain unchanged. A breakfast cup is a little larger than a standard cup; about 280ml or 1/2 pint. A teacup is smaller than a standard cup; about 140ml or 1/4 pint (similar to 1 gill). A rough conversion is:

1 breakfast cup = 1 standard cup + 2 tablespoons
1 teacup = ½ standard cup + 1 tablespoon

Here are some common breakfast cup and teacup measurements and their approximate gram equivalents.

| Ingredient | 1 breakfast cup | 1 teacup |
|---|---|---|
| flour | 160g | 80g |
| mixed fruit | 150g | 75g |
| sugar | 250g | 125g |
| brown sugar | 230g | 115g |

## Temperatures

Oven temperatures are often not given in Celsius or Fahrenheit but described as 'a quick oven' or 'a slow oven'. For today's cook, cooking in a modern oven, these descriptions have been converted as follows:

| | |
|---|---|
| slow oven | 120°C |
| moderate oven | 180°C |
| quick oven | 220°C |

## Cooking times

In Aunt Daisy's recipes cooking times were frequently omitted. These have been added to most recipes to make life easier for the modern cook. However, ovens and oven temperatures vary widely, so even where cooking times are given, it is recommended to test for doneness during the cooking process.

Heavier cakes and puddings are cooked when a skewer pushed into the centre comes out clean. Lighter cakes are cooked if they spring back when pushed gently with your finger.

## Bakeware

The recipes in this book rarely mention the size of baking tins, so some common sense and guesswork is required. For cakes, the tin should be half to two-thirds full of batter. If the tin is too full, the batter may over flow. If there is not enough batter in the tin, the cake will shrink around the edges.

As a general guide, a 23cm round or 23cm square cake tin will take 5 cups of cake batter, a 23cm ring tin will take 4 cups, and a 23cm x 14cm loaf tin will take 4 cups.

# Biscuits &
# Small Cakes

# Afghans

| | |
|---|---|
| 170g butter | pinch of salt |
| 85g sugar | 1 tablespoon cocoa |
| 170g flour | 60g cornflakes |

Cream butter and sugar.
Add dry ingredients.
Roll into balls and cook on a cold tray in a moderate oven
(180°C) for about 15 minutes.

## Variation:

Substitute 60g cornflour for cornflakes, or 30g cornflour and
2 tablespoons cornflakes. Add about 2 tablespoons boiling
water when creaming butter and sugar. When cold, ice with
chocolate icing, and put a piece of walnut on top.

# Almond Shortbread

| | |
|---|---|
| 285g butter | 30g ground almonds |
| 115g icing sugar | 285g flour |
| 30g cornflour | salt |

Cream butter and sugar together, gradually adding dry
ingredients.
Work into a firm smooth paste.
Roll out evenly on a baking sheet, or cut into shapes as
required.
Cook in a moderate oven (180°C) for 20 minutes or
until golden.

Almond Shortbread, page 8

# Almond Fingers

115g flour
¼ teaspoon baking powder
good pinch of salt
60g butter
115g sugar

38g ground almonds
1 egg yolk, beaten
1 egg white, beaten
60g icing sugar
30g chopped almonds

Sift flour, baking powder and salt.
Rub in butter, add sugar and ground almonds and mix with egg yolk to a stiff paste.
Roll out oblong on a floured board.
Mix egg white and icing sugar.
Spread over paste and sprinkle chopped almonds over. Cut into fingers.
Bake on a greased tray in a moderate oven (180°C) for 10 to 15 minutes.

# Anzac Biscuits

115g butter
1 tablespoon golden syrup
1 teaspoon baking
   powder dissolved in 2
   tablespoons boiling water

1 cup sugar
1 cup coconut
1 cup wheatmeal
1 cup chopped walnuts
¾ cup flour

Melt butter with golden syrup.
Add baking powder. Add all other ingredients.
Take small teaspoonfuls and roll into balls.
Place on a cold oven sheet, leaving space between each.
Cook for 30 minutes in a slow oven (120°C).

# Aotea Date Kisses

450g butter
340g sugar
4 egg yolks
45g cocoa

790g flour
1 teaspoon baking powder
4 egg whites, beaten
dates

Cream butter and sugar.
Add egg yolks then cocoa.
Add sifted flour and baking powder.
Mix well and roll into little balls.
Press a date in centre. Brush with egg white.
Cook in a moderate oven (180°C) for 15 to 20 minutes.
Makes about 84 kisses.

# Biffs

85g butter
½ breakfast cup brown sugar
1 egg
1 breakfast cup cornflakes
½ teaspoon baking powder

¼ teaspoon vanilla essence
½ cup walnuts
1 salt spoon of salt
1 teacup flour

Mix into a firm dough and shape into rounds.
Place on greased trays and bake in a moderate oven (180°C)
    for 15 to 20 minutes.

# Brian O'Brien's Bran Biscuits

115g butter
1 cup sugar
1 cup flour

1 heaped cup bran
1 teaspoon baking powder
1 egg

Cream butter and sugar.
Mix in other ingredients.
Roll out and cut into rounds.
Bake on a greased oven tray at 180°C for 15 minutes.

# Bumble Bees

1 cup chopped dates
½ cup walnuts
½ cup preserved ginger
½ cup figs

1 cup sultanas or raisins
1 cup coconut
1 small tin sweetened
    condensed milk

Mix all together and squeeze into oval shapes.
Put on a greased tray and bake in a moderate oven (180°C)
    until golden.

# Cheese Biscuits

115g butter
170g flour
60g finely grated cheese

½ teaspoon baking powder
salt and pepper
a little cold milk to mix

Rub butter into flour.
Add cheese, baking powder, and salt and pepper.
Mix to a stiff paste with milk and roll to 3mm thick.
Cut into shapes.
Bake in a hot oven (220°C) for 7 to 10 minutes until golden
    brown.

# Cheese Cakes

115g butter
115g sugar
2 eggs
140g flour

1 teaspoon baking powder
115g flaky pastry
a little raspberry jam

Cream butter and sugar.
Beat eggs and add alternately with sifted flour and baking
    powder.
Roll out pastry and line about 21 patty tins.
Put 1 teaspoon raspberry jam on bottom of each, then
    1 large spoonful of cake mixture on top. Place a small
    strip of pastry on top.
Bake about 20 minutes at 200°C.

# Chocolate Chinese Chews

¼ cup melted butter
1 cup sugar
2 eggs
2 tablespoons milk
1 cup flour

1 teaspoon baking powder
2 tablespoons cocoa
1 teaspoon vanilla essence
1 cup chopped walnuts
1 cup chopped dates

Beat butter and sugar.
Add eggs one by one then milk.
Sift in flour, baking powder, cocoa and essence. Add nuts
    and dates.
Spread in pan 6mm thick.
Bake at 190°C for about 20 minutes. When cooked,
    cut into squares.

# Chocolate Fingers

225g flour
85g butter
85g sugar
1 egg yolk
1 dessertspoon cocoa

1 teaspoon baking powder
icing made with white of egg
    and icing sugar
chopped walnuts

Mix all together (except last 2 ingredients) like shortbread.
Roll out and cut into fingers.
Bake in a steady oven (about 180°C).
Spread with icing. Sprinkle with walnuts.

# Chocolate Roughs

1 egg
pinch of salt
¾ cup brown sugar
1 tablespoon butter
1 tablespoon cocoa

1 tablespoon boiling water
1 teaspoon vanilla essence
1 cup coconut
1 large cup rolled oats

Beat egg with salt and sugar until thick.
Melt butter and cocoa in boiling water and add.
Stir in vanilla, coconut and rolled oats.
Place small heaps on a greased tray and cook about
    30 minutes in a moderate oven (180°C).

# Coconut Fudge Biscuits

1 cup flour
115g coconut
115g sugar

1 tablespoon cocoa
115g butter, melted
½ teaspoon vanilla essence

Put all dry ingredients into a basin and pour over
    melted butter and vanilla essence.
Mix until like breadcrumbs.
Press into a sponge roll or sandwich tin.
Bake at 180°C until set. Cut while warm.
This is good for cooking in oven after cooking dinner.

# Cornflake Meringues

2 egg whites
½ cup sugar
¼ teaspoon vanilla essence
½ teaspoon vinegar

pinch of salt
2 cups cornflakes
½ cup chopped walnuts

Beat egg whites until stiff.
Add other ingredients and mix.
Place teaspoonfuls on a cold greased tray and bake at 120°C
for 1½ hours.

# Eltham Ginger Nuts

1.15kg flour
450g light brown sugar
30g ground ginger

225g butter
900g golden syrup, warmed

Rub dry ingredients together well.
Beat in the butter. Mix with sufficient syrup to make
a stiff dough.
Make into little marbles by rolling pieces of dough into thin
strips, chopping bits off (as though chopping rhubarb).
Roll each one into a little marble. Flatten slightly.
Bake for 15 minutes or less at 190°C. No rising.

# Fruit Nut Marshmallows

½ cup cornflour
1 breakfast cup wholemeal
flour
2 level teaspoons baking
powder
½ teaspoon salt
½ cup brown sugar

115g melted butter
1 egg, beaten
milk to mix
minced sultanas
walnuts
honey

## Marshmallow

2 teaspoons gelatine
½ cup hot water
1 egg white, beaten

lemon essence
1 cup icing sugar
walnut halves

Sift flours, baking powder and salt and mix with sugar.
Add butter, egg and enough milk to make a stiff mixture.
Roll out thin and put on cold greased trays. Mark into
squares.
Cook about 15 minutes at 230°C.
When cold, stick two together with a layer of sultanas and
walnuts, blended with honey.

To make the marshmallow, dissolve gelatine in hot water.
Let it cool.
Add egg white, lemon essence and icing sugar.
Beat and beat until white and thick and creamy.
Spread on top of biscuits and finish with half a walnut.

Aotea Date Kisses, page 10

# Gems

| | |
|---|---|
| 2 eggs | 1 cup milk |
| ½ cup sugar | 2 cups flour |
| 30g butter, melted | 3 teaspoons baking powder |

Beat eggs and sugar very well.
Add butter. Add milk then other ingredients.
Have gem irons very hot and grease with butter or oil.
Half fill with mixture and cook in a hot oven (220°C).
Makes 24 gems.

# Ginger Nuts

| | |
|---|---|
| 72g butter | 1 dessertspoon ground ginger |
| ½ cup golden syrup | ¼ teaspoon baking soda |
| 225g flour | pinch of salt |

Melt butter and syrup.
Add other ingredients. Mix to a stiff paste.
Roll out on a floured board. Cut into rounds.
Put on a greased baking tray. Bake in a moderate oven
(180°C) for about 15 minutes.

# Hokey Pokey Biscuits

1 dessertspoon golden
   syrup
1 dessertspoon milk
1 teaspoon baking soda

115g butter
½ to ¾ cup sugar
1 large cup flour

Melt syrup and milk together.
When nearly cold, add baking soda and beat until frothy.
Cream butter and sugar. Add frothy mixture, then the flour.
Roll into balls, place on a greased baking tray and press
   with a fork.
Cook in a slow oven (120°C) for about 30 minutes.

# Honey Raisin Cakes

60g butter
30g caster sugar
30g honey
1 egg

85g flour
½ teaspoon baking powder
1 dessertspoon milk
60g chopped raisins

Cream butter, sugar and honey.
Add egg and beat very well. Stir in other ingredients.
Cook in greased patty tins for about 20 minutes in a
   medium oven (180°C).
60g honey may replace the honey and caster sugar.

# Jelly Cakes

½ cup butter
½ cup sugar
2 eggs, well beaten
1 cup flour
1 teaspoon baking powder

a little milk
essence of choice
1 packet red jelly crystals
coconut

Cream butter and sugar.
Add eggs then flour sifted with baking powder.
Add milk and essence.
Place in patty tins or paper cases and bake until golden.
Make up the jelly, and when nearly set, dip cakes in, then
    roll in coconut.

# Kiwi Biscuits

115g butter
¼ cup sugar
2 tablespoons sweetened
    condensed milk
1 cup flour

1 teaspoon baking powder
pinch of salt
1 cake of dairy chocolate,
    chopped into pieces the
    size of a pea

Cream butter and sugar. Add condensed milk.
Sift in flour, baking powder and salt. Stir in chocolate.
Roll into little balls and place on a cold tray. Press down
    with a fork dipped in boiling water.
Cook in a very moderate oven (160°C).

# Maori Kisses – Eggless

2 heaped tablespoons butter
4 tablespoons sugar
very little milk
1 cup flour, sieved
1 tablespoon cocoa
1 teaspoon baking powder
½ cup chopped walnuts
¾ cup chopped dates
¼ cup preserved ginger
a few drops of vanilla essence

## Caramel Icing

2 tablespoons milk
5 tablespoons brown sugar
3 tablespoons butter

Melt butter and add sugar, milk, flour, cocoa, baking
    powder, nuts, fruits and essence.
Make into small teaspoon-sized balls.
Cook on a cold tray neither greased nor floured.
Cook at 190°C for 10 to 15 minutes.
Join when cold with vanilla butter icing (see filling for
    Melting Moments, page 21), or make bigger and ice
    separately with caramel icing.

To make caramel icing, bring to the boil for 3 or 4 minutes.
Beat until thick. Takes 10 to 20 minutes to beat.

# Melting Moments

115g butter
30g icing sugar
60g flour

60g cornflour
½ teaspoon baking powder

## Filling

115g icing sugar
vanilla essence
a walnut-sized piece of butter

Cream butter and sugar and work in other ingredients.
Bake in small lots in a moderate oven (180°C) for about
15 minutes.
Stick together with icing filling.
To make the filling, mix ingredients well with a little cold water.

# Meringues

2 egg whites
115g caster sugar
pinch of salt

1 level teaspoon baking
powder
a little extra caster sugar

Whip egg whites until they won't fall out of a basin
when inverted.
Gently whip in half the sugar with a pinch of salt,
a little at a time.
When stiff again, gently fold in the rest of the sugar and the
baking powder.
Put dessertspoonfuls on baking paper laid on greased
oven tray.
Sprinkle with extra sugar.
Takes 1½ to 2 hours in a very cool oven (120°C).

# Nougatines ~ French

## Pastry

115g flour, sifted
72g butter
cold water

## Filling

60g butter
60g caster sugar
1 egg
30g ground almonds
30g sponge cake crumbs

a few drops almond essence
jam
2 tablespoons whole
   almonds, blanched and
   chopped finely

## Pastry

Rub flour with butter until it resembles fine breadcrumbs.
Add sufficient cold water until mixed to a stiff paste.
Grease some fluted patty tins.
Roll out pastry to rather less than 6mm, cut into rounds,
   and line bottom and sides of pans with pastry. Trim
   around top edge to make even.

## Filling

Cream butter and sugar.
Quickly stir in egg, and beat well for a few minutes.
Add ground almonds and sponge cake crumbs. Mix
   thoroughly then mix in essence.
Put enough jam into bottom of each patty tin to cover.
Fill pans three-quarters full with mixture. Sprinkle top with
   chopped almonds.
Bake in a moderate oven (180°C) for about 20 minutes.
   Place on a sieve to cool.

# Novelty Biscuits

2 breakfast cups coconut
1 breakfast cup chopped
　raisins and sultanas mixed
1 breakfast cup chopped
　dates

1 breakfast cup chopped
　walnuts
1 tin sweetened condensed
　milk

Mix all together and make small balls about the size of a
　walnut.
Bake on greased oven shelf very slowly for 15 minutes (120°C).
Pack in a tin — will keep a long time.
Can halve or double this quantity. No flour, butter,
　sugar or eggs.

# Old-fashioned Brandy Snaps

170g butter
170g golden syrup
170g sugar
2 teaspoons ground ginger

½ teaspoon lemon essence
½ teaspoon vanilla
170g flour

Put all ingredients except flour into a saucepan and allow to
　warm slightly until butter is melted.
Mix in flour.
Drop small teaspoonfuls on a greased oven tray, leaving
　plenty of room to spread.
Bake at 180°C for about 10 minutes.

# Overnight Biscuits

| | |
|---|---|
| 115g butter | 1 teaspoon baking soda |
| ¾ cup sugar | ½ cup walnuts |
| 1 egg | ½ cup cherries |
| 1 tablespoon treacle | ½ cup preserved ginger |
| 1½ cups flour | |

Cream butter and sugar.
Add egg and all other ingredients.
Form into 2 pats like butter and leave all night.
Cut very thin next day, and cook in a slow oven (120°C).

# Peanut Butter Lunch Cookies

| | |
|---|---|
| 1½ cups sweetened condensed milk | ½ cup peanut butter |
| | 3 cups shredded coconut |

Mix and drop in spoonfuls on a greased baking sheet.
Bake for 15 minutes at 190°C, or until brown, about
30 minutes.

# Handy Hint

**Teacups, Stained —**
Rub with a cloth dipped in vinegar and salt.

**Teapots, Aluminium —**
Clean the inside frequently with half a lemon dipped in salt.

ocolate Fingers, page 13

Cornflake Meringues, page 15

# Peanut Cookies

115g butter
1 teacup brown sugar
1 egg
1 dessertspoon cocoa
1 salt spoon of salt

1 teacup wheat flakes
1 teaspoon baking powder
1 level cup flour
225g roasted peanuts

Cream butter and sugar. Break in egg.
Add cocoa, then other dry ingredients, then peanuts.
Place in rocky pieces on greased scone trays and bake in a
moderate oven (180°C).

# Richmond Maids of Honour

1 teacup cream
150g butter
1 boiled floury potato
4 egg yolks
30g ground almonds
1 tablespoon lemon juice
150g sugar

30g minced nuts
grated rind of 2 lemons
a little nutmeg
2 tablespoons brandy
    (or hot water flavoured
    with brandy essence)
puff pastry

Mix cream gradually into soft butter.
Rub potato to a smooth flour and add to cream mixture.
Beat in egg yolks.
Mix in all other ingredients.
Line patty tins with puff pastry and half fill with mixture.
Bake at 180°C for 20 minutes.

# Spiders – No Cooking

225g vegetable shortening
4 cups corn or wheat flakes
1 cup icing sugar
½ teaspoon vanilla essence

1 cup coconut
4 tablespoons cocoa
1 cup raisins (if desired)

Melt shortening, and pour over dry ingredients. Mix well.
Press into a flat tin and set aside to cool.
Cut when cold or put in teaspoon lots on baking
    paper to set.
Leave overnight to set.

# Sponge Cakes – Gem Iron

3 small or 2 large eggs
1 cup sugar
1 cup flour
1 teaspoon baking powder

1 dessertspoon butter
    dissolved in ½ cup
    boiling water
pinch of salt
vanilla or lemon essence

Beat eggs, and add sugar until creamy as for sponge.
Sift flour and baking powder and fold in very lightly.
Add butter and water, salt and essence. Stir slightly.
Have gem irons very hot (as for gems) and butter them well.
    Fill about three-quarters full.
They only take 5 or 6 minutes to cook.
This quantity makes about 36 little sponges.
(If a good pinch of salt is added to eggs and they are beaten
    well before adding sugar, it will not take as long to beat
    the eggs and sugar creamy.)

# Stuffed Monkeys

| | |
|---|---|
| 340g butter | 15g cinnamon |
| 225g sugar | 1 egg |
| 450g flour | |

## Filling Mixture

| | |
|---|---|
| 115g sultanas or raisins | ½ cup dates |
| 115g lemon peel, cut small | cinnamon or mixed spice |
| 30g chopped walnuts | to taste |

Mix and roll out thin. Cut in rounds.
Put filling mixture between 2 rounds and pinch together.
Bake in a moderate oven (180°C).

# Tango Cakes

| | |
|---|---|
| 60g butter | 1 tablespoon cocoa |
| 1 cup sugar | vanilla essence |
| 1 egg, beaten | 115g chopped dates |
| 1 large cup flour | 115g chopped walnuts |
| 2 tablespoons cornflour | walnut halves |
| 1 teaspoon baking powder | |

Cream butter and sugar. Add egg.
Sift flour, cornflour, baking powder and cocoa.
Stir into butter and sugar with vanilla. Add dates and walnuts.
Bake in paper cases for 10 minutes in a hot oven (220°C).
Ice with icing made from icing sugar and cocoa dissolved in
    a little boiling water.
Place walnut half on top of each.
These are nice economical little cakes.
Makes about 20 to 24.

# Teddies

| | |
|---|---|
| 1 small tin sweetened condensed milk | 1 cup chopped dates |
| 1 cup chopped walnuts | 1 cup coconut |

Mix together milk, walnuts and dates. Roll in coconut.
Bake on a greased tray in a moderate oven (180°C) for
10 to 15 minutes.

# Trifle Cakes

| | |
|---|---|
| 85g wholemeal flour | ½ teaspoon baking powder |
| 85g flour | 1 egg yolk |
| 85g butter | raspberry jam |
| 60g brown sugar | whipped cream to serve |
| ½ teaspoon mixed spice | |

## Filling

| | |
|---|---|
| 3 tablespoons cake crumbs | a little brandy or brandy essence |
| 2 tablespoons sultanas | 2 dessertspoons raspberry jam |

Make biscuit pastry with wholemeal flour, flour, butter,
    brown sugar, spice, baking powder and egg yolk.
Line patty tins and bake at 190°C for 15 minutes.
When cooked put a layer of jam in the bottom and fill with
    filling.
Top with a little whipped cream.

# Walnut Crisps

115g butter
115g sugar
1 egg
60g flour
4 teaspoons cocoa

1 teaspoon baking powder
½ cup chopped walnuts
170g fine wholemeal flour
vanilla essence

Cream butter and sugar. Add egg and other ingredients.
Spread 3mm thick on bottom of a shallow tin.
Bake in a slow oven (120°C) for 30 to 45 minutes.
Cut into squares while hot.

# Walnut Wafers

2 eggs
1 cup brown sugar
¼ teaspoon salt

1 cup chopped almonds and
   walnuts mixed
vanilla essence
3½ tablespoons flour

Beat eggs and sugar well.
Add salt, nuts and essence, and mix well.
Add flour and beat well again.
Cut out and bake in a moderate oven (180°C) until a nice
   golden colour.

# Wienco Torte

4 tablespoons finely
   chopped nuts
1 teaspoon baking soda
2 teaspoons cream of tartar
2¼ tablespoons butter
4 tablespoons icing sugar

3 egg yolks, well beaten
4 tablespoons flour
3 egg whites, stiffly beaten
raspberry or strawberry jam
chocolate icing

Mix together nuts, baking soda and cream of tartar.
Cream butter and icing sugar with egg yolks.
Add flour and then egg whites.
(A little hot water or milk may be necessary to make the
   cake the usual sponge-sandwich consistency.)
Bake in sandwich tins for about 15 minutes. Put together
   with jam and ice with chocolate icing.

# Yo Yo Biscuits

170g plain flour
60g custard powder
pinch of salt

170g butter
60g icing sugar
butter icing (see page 141)

Sift flour, custard powder and salt.
Cream butter and icing sugar. Blend both mixtures.
Make into balls, put on a greased oven tray, and press with
   a fork.
Bake until pale golden brown (at 180°C for about
   15 minutes).
Put together in pairs with butter icing.

# Large Cakes

# Almond Cake

60g butter
85g sugar
60g ground almonds
60g cake crumbs
60g plain flour

30g cornflour
2 eggs, beaten
½ teaspoon almond essence
½ teaspoon baking powder

Cream butter and sugar thoroughly. Add almonds and
   cake crumbs.
Sift flour and cornflour together, and add alternately with
   eggs, beating all well.
Add almond essence and baking powder.
Turn into a greased sandwich tin.
Bake at about 200°C for 20 to 30 minutes.

# Almond Madeira

225g butter
225g sugar
4 eggs
170g flour

170g ground almonds
1 teaspoon baking powder
1 teaspoon salt

Cream butter and sugar.
Add eggs, then sifted dry ingredients.
Bake in a deep tin at 180°C for about 1½ hours.
(To make this into Sand Cake, use half cornflour and half
   ordinary flour.)
Ice with plain icing mixed with almond essence. Then
   decorate with a small piece of maidenhair fern in one
   corner, and little knobs of yellow icing to imitate
   wattle blossom.

Ginger Nuts, page 17

# Angel Cake

⅔ cup milk
¾ cup sugar
⅛ teaspoon salt
2 egg whites
1 cup flour
1 teaspoon baking powder
½ teaspoon cream of tartar
½ teaspoon almond essence
½ teaspoon vanilla essence
icing (if desired)

Heat milk and sugar just to boil.
Add salt to egg whites and beat stiff.
Add milk and sugar slowly to egg whites, beating
    continually. Let cool.
Sift together 5 times: flour, baking powder and cream of tartar.
Fold into egg mixture. Add essences.
Pour into a small ungreased angel cake tin.
Bake at 180°C for about 30 minutes.
Remove from oven. Invert pan and allow to stand until cold.
Cover top and sides with icing if desired.
Note: Excellent to make with the Gold Cake (see page 61).
    Only 3 eggs are required for both.

# Apple Cake

½ cup butter
1 breakfast cup brown sugar
2 eggs, well beaten
1½ cups flour
1 teaspoon baking soda
1 teaspoon mixed spice
½ cup raisins
½ cup walnuts
1 cup thinly sliced apples
1 tablespoon sugar
pinch of cinnamon
1 tablespoon brown sugar
a little cinnamon and nutmeg

Cream butter and sugar. Add eggs.

Add flour sifted with baking soda and spices. Stir in raisins and nuts.

Place half mixture into a prepared tin.

Add apples sprinkled with the 1 tablespoon sugar and cinnamon. Add remaining mixture.

Put in a good oven (180°C) for about 1 hour.

When nearly cooked, sprinkle top of cake with 1 tablespoon brown sugar.

Put greased paper on top so sugar won't burn. Take off just before taking cake from oven.

Keep 2 or 3 days before cutting.

If preferred, raisins and nuts may be omitted.

# Apple Fruit Cake

1 tablespoon butter
1½ cups stewed apple sweetened with
    ½ cup sugar
1 cup brown sugar
1 tablespoon cocoa
1 dessertspoon mixed spice
½ teaspoon baking soda
2 large cups flour
about 1½ cups lemon peel and dried fruits to taste
a little milk (if necessary)

Melt butter into apple and sugar. Mix together all other
    ingredients.
Add apple mixture and a little milk if needed.
Line a tin with greased paper.
Bake in a moderate oven (180°C) for about 1½ hours.
Do not cut this cake for a fortnight.

# Handy Hint

**Fruit Cakes, Dry —**

To prevent, add 1 small minced apple to a large cake before baking. Dry cakes
are the result of over-cooking or using too much flour.

After baking:

1.    Put a piece of apple or potato in the cake tin.
2.    Pour a nip of brandy into the tin, and stand cake in this for a
      few hours.
3.    Make holes in the bottom of the cake with fine knitting needles.
      Gently pour in 1 tbsp glycerine.
4.    Wrap cake in a teatowel which has been wrung out of boiling water,
      and leave for a few hours.

# Apple Meringue Cake

½ cup vegetable shortening
1 cup brown sugar
2 egg yolks, unbeaten
2 cups flour, sifted
1 teaspoon baking soda
¼ teaspoon salt
1 teaspoon cinnamon
½ teaspoon cloves
½ teaspoon nutmeg
1 cup thick, unsweetened apple sauce

## Meringue

2 egg whites
½ cup brown sugar
½ cup chopped nuts

Cream shortening and sugar. Add egg yolks and blend well.
Sift flour, baking soda, salt and spices well together.
Add to creamed mixture alternately with the apple sauce.
Pour into a greased pan (20cm x 30cm), lined with
    baking paper.
Top with meringue.

To make the meringue, beat egg whites until stiff.
Gradually add sugar and beat until mixture peaks.
Spread over raw batter. Sprinkle with chopped nuts.
Bake in a moderate oven (180°C) for about 30 minutes.

# Banana Sponge

115g butter
1 teacup sugar
1 egg, well beaten
1½ cups flour
1 teaspoon baking powder
3 firm bananas, mashed
1 teaspoon baking soda dissolved in 2 tablespoons milk
mock cream or real cream to serve

Cream butter and sugar. Add egg, then flour, baking powder
 and bananas.
Add soda in milk.
Bake in a moderate oven (180°C) for 30 minutes.
This sponge can be baked either in sandwich tins and mock
 cream filling put between, or in a flat baking tin with
 whipped cream on top.

# Handy Hint

**Cream, to Whip —**
1.  If cream is difficult to whip, add 1 egg white, and stand basin in a
    vessel of cold water for 1 hour before whipping. This also increases
    the amount without flavouring the cream.
2.  If cream goes watery, dissolve a little gelatine in 2 tsp water and
    whip in.

# Battenburg Cake

| | |
|---|---|
| 4 tablespoons butter | ½ cup milk |
| ¾ cup sugar | ½ teaspoon vanilla |
| 2 cups flour | 2 egg whites, beaten stiff |
| 2 teaspoons baking powder | pink food colouring |
| ½ teaspoon salt | strawberry filling |

## Strawberry Filling

| | |
|---|---|
| 2 tablespoons strawberry jam | 1 teaspoon melted butter |
| 1 cup sifted icing sugar | hot water |

## Coconut Paste

| | |
|---|---|
| 1 tablespoon butter | ¼ teaspoon almond essence |
| 1½ cups sifted icing sugar | green food colouring |
| ⅛ teaspoon salt | ½ cup desiccated coconut |
| 2 tablespoons lemon juice | |

Cream the butter. Add sugar gradually and beat until light and fluffy.

Sift flour with baking powder and salt. Add alternately with milk.

Add vanilla. Fold in egg whites.

Divide batter into two and colour one half pink.

Bake in 2 greased square sandwich tins in a moderate oven (180°C) for about 20 minutes.

Cool. Cut each into 6 even strips. Join layers like a chequerboard, with strawberry filling.

Cover outside with coconut paste.

Leave in a cool place for 24 hours.

To make the strawberry filling, beat jam into icing sugar.
Add butter and sufficient hot water to make a smooth
spreading paste.

To make the coconut paste, cream butter, icing sugar, salt
and lemon juice.
Add sufficient hot water to make a smooth paste.
Add almond essence and green colouring. Add coconut and
beat well.
Should be as thick as possible. Spread evenly on cake.

# Block Cake

| | |
|---|---|
| 225g butter | 115g cherries |
| 2 heaped cups flour | 85g peel |
| 1 cup sugar | 450g sultanas |
| 2 eggs, well beaten | 1½ teaspoons vanilla |
| 1 cup boiling milk | essence |
| 85g almonds | 1 teaspoon baking soda |
| 450g raisins | dissolved in a little milk |

Rub butter well into flour until it resembles crumbs. Add
sugar and mix.
Mix eggs and milk.
Put in a saucepan and let get very hot until like a custard.
Do not let boil or you will have a curdled mixture —
just very hot.
Take off heat and let cool, but not too cold.
Add nuts, fruit and essence to mixture.
Pour custard into mix. Stir well until blended. Add soda.
Bake in a square tin in a moderate oven (180°C) for about
2 hours.
If a dark cake is required, put in 1 tablespoon blackcurrant
jam, but very nice as it is.

# Californian Orange Sponge Cake

3 egg whites
pinch of cream of tartar
3 egg yolks
1 cup sugar
½ cup orange juice
2 teaspoons grated orange rind

1½ cups flour
1½ teaspoons baking powder
pinch of salt
white frosting to decorate
orange rind to decorate

## Filling

¼ cup sugar
1 tablespoon flour
pinch of salt

1 egg yolk
1 dessertspoon butter
1 teaspoon lemon juice

Whip egg whites and cream of tartar until stiff.

Beat in egg yolks, one at a time.

Add sugar gradually, beating vigorously.

Add orange juice and rind. Fold in lightly with sifted flour, baking powder and salt.

Bake in 2 layer cake pans in a moderate oven for about 10 minutes.

Ice cake with white icing (see page 155) and sprinkle with grated orange rind.

To make the filling, mix all ingredients (except lemon juice) together and cook in a double boiler until smooth and thick.

Remove from heat and add lemon juice.

Wienco Torte, page 30

# Californian Prune Cake

2 eggs, beaten
1 cup sour milk
1 cup sugar
1½ cups flour
1 teaspoon cinnamon

1 teaspoon baking soda
⅓ cup melted butter
1 cup chopped pitted prunes
1 cup chopped nuts
½ teaspoon vanilla essence

Add eggs to milk and sifted dry ingredients.
Add butter. Add prunes, nuts and vanilla.
If more moisture is needed, add prune juice.
Bake in a moderate oven (180°C).
[Note: plain unsweetened yoghurt can be used instead of
sour milk.]

# Canadian Date Cake

1 breakfast cup sugar
225g butter
2 eggs, beaten
1 teaspoon baking soda
    dissolved in ¾ cup
    cold water

1 breakfast cup dates
1 breakfast cup walnuts
1 tablespoon maple or
    golden syrup
2 breakfast cups flour

Cream butter and sugar. Add eggs.
Dissolve soda in water and pour over dates. Let it stand
    1 hour.
Add to creamed sugar. Add nuts.
Mix in syrup and flour.
Bake 1½ hours in a moderate oven (180°C) in a tin lined
    with buttered paper.

# Canadian Orange Cake

½ cup butter
1 cup sugar
2 eggs, beaten well
1 teaspoon vanilla essence
1 teaspoon baking soda
   dissolved in ¾ cup
   warm water

½ teaspoon salt sifted with
   2 cups flour
1 whole seedless orange
   (skin and all)
1 cup raisins
½ cup walnuts

Cream butter. Add sugar, eggs, vanilla, baking soda, salt
   and flour. Beat well.
Mince orange, raisins and walnuts in a mincer.
Add to mixture and beat well.
Bake at 180°C for approximately 50 minutes.

# Chocolate Cake

1 tablespoon butter
½ cup brown sugar
1 tablespoon golden syrup
1 egg
½ teaspoon baking soda
   dissolved in ½ cup milk

1 cup flour
1 teaspoon baking powder
1 tablespoon cocoa
icing and chopped nuts
   to serve

Cream butter and sugar. Add syrup and egg, then milk with
   baking soda dissolved in it.
Add flour, baking powder and cocoa.
Bake in one tin at 190°C for about 30 minutes. Ice and
   sprinkle with chopped nuts.

For Coffee Cake: Substitute 1 tablespoon coffee essence for
   cocoa, and add 2 extra tablespoons flour.

# Foolproof Chocolate Cake

115g butter
1 teacup sugar
1 egg
2 tablespoons golden syrup, melted
2 cups flour
2 tablespoons cocoa
1 teaspoon baking soda dissolved in 1 cup milk
1 teaspoon baking powder

Beat butter, sugar and egg. Add syrup.
Sift flour and cocoa together. Add soda in milk and beat
    well until smooth and light.
Add baking powder.
Bake in a moderate oven (180°C) for about 45 minutes in a
    tin about 30cm x 20cm.
Keeps well.

# Handy Hint

**Egg economy —**

1.  Grated carrot is a good substitute for eggs in boiled puddings.
2.  A little vinegar containing a little bicarbonate of soda may be used in
    cakes when eggs are scarce. Allow 1 dssp vinegar with ½ tsp of the
    baking soda for every 2 eggs, and add this last.
3.  When beating 'separated' eggs, add 1 tsp of golden syrup to the
    yolk. One egg will thus go almost as far as three.
4.  Add 1 tsp of vinegar instead of one of the eggs required when
    making a cake.

# Special Chocolate Cake

4 tablespoons butter
4 tablespoons sugar
2 eggs
6 tablespoons milk
6 tablespoons flour

2 tablespoons ground rice
2 teaspoons baking powder
2 tablespoons cocoa

## Filling

1½ tablespoons butter
icing sugar
½ cup strong cocoa made
    with milk

a little vanilla essence
chopped walnuts

Beat butter and sugar to a cream. Add eggs and beat well.
    Add milk.
Sift dry ingredients together and add.
Bake in 2 flat tins for about 20 minutes at 180°C.
To make the filling, beat butter to a cream with icing sugar.
Beat in cocoa. Add vanilla essence.
Put filling between cake, and on top.
Top with chopped walnuts.

# Chocolate Roll

3 egg yolks
1 teacup caster sugar
2 tablespoons warm water
1 teacup flour

½ teaspoon baking powder
3 teaspoons cocoa
3 egg whites, stiffly beaten

Line a Swiss roll tin with greased paper.
Beat egg yolks and sugar in a basin over a pan of water
    until thick and creamy. Add water.
Stir sifted flour, baking powder and cocoa in lightly. Fold in
    egg whites.
Pour into a prepared tin.
Bake about 12 to 15 minutes at about 180°C.
Turn onto sugared paper, roll up and hold 1 minute. Unroll.
Spread with warm raspberry or apricot jam. Roll up again.

# Coffee Cake

85g butter
170g sugar
3 eggs
1 tablespoon coffee essence
½ teaspoon vanilla essence

125g flour
1 teaspoon baking powder
3 tablespoons cornflour
3 tablespoons milk

Cream butter and sugar. Beat in eggs and essences.
Sift together dry ingredients. Add to butter mixture
    alternately with milk.
Place in cake tin and bake for about 40 minutes at 180°C.

# Christmas Cake

| | |
|---|---|
| 450g fruit (or more) | 3 eggs |
| 1 cup hot water | 1 tablespoon golden syrup |
| 115g butter | 1½ cups flour |
| 1 cup sugar (brown preferred) | 1 teaspoon baking powder |
| | essence (if liked) |

Simmer fruit in water until all water is absorbed. Allow to cool.
Cream butter and sugar, add eggs and syrup, then the flour, baking powder and fruit.
Bake approximately 1½ hours in moderate oven (180°C).
For a larger cake, double quantities.

# £100 Prize Christmas Cake

| | |
|---|---|
| 60g candied peel | 450g sugar |
| grated rind of 1 orange | 8 eggs |
| grated rind and juice 1 lemon | 565g flour, sifted |
| 2 tablespoons orange marmalade | ½ teaspoon baking powder |
| ½ cup brandy | 1 salt spoon of salt |
| 170g blanched almonds | 675g sultanas |
| 450g butter | 225g raisins |
| | 450g currants |
| | 115g glacé cherries |

## Icing
450g icing sugar
115g ground almonds
1 egg yolk
2 teaspoons lemon juice and water
1 egg white, beaten

# Royal Icing

225g icing sugar
1 egg white
squeeze of lemon

Mix peel, orange and lemon rinds, and marmalade, place in
a bowl and pour over lemon juice and brandy.

Cut almonds in two lengthways.

Cover tightly and leave overnight.

Blend butter and sugar until quite smooth.

Add eggs, one at a time, using a little flour to prevent
curdling.

Mix flour with baking powder and salt.

Add fruit mixture and flour mixture, a little at a time,
to egg mixture.

Have oven tin ready with four layers of paper lining.

Pour in mixture, hollow slightly, and bake slowly (120°C)
for 6 hours.

When thoroughly cool, wrap in baking paper and leave for
3 weeks before cutting.

Ice 1 week before cutting.

## Icing

Sift icing sugar and mix with ground almonds.

Add egg yolk and lemon juice and water.

Keep it stiff and knead well.

Roll out to fit cake and brush cake with egg white.

Brush crumbs off cake, press icing gently on to it, and allow
to stand 2 days before covering with royal icing.

## Royal Icing

Mix icing sugar with egg white and lemon.

Make very stiff and spread on cake with a knife dipped in
hot water.

Decorate according to taste.

# 12R Special Christmas Cake

900g fruit
285g flour, sifted
225g butter
225g sugar
5 eggs
½ teaspoon each of essence of: vanilla, lemon, pineapple,
    brandy, cherry, almond or any other of choice
¼ to ½ teaspoon curry powder
1 teaspoon baking powder

Prepare fruit and sprinkle with a little flour.
Place in a warm place while creaming butter and sugar.
    Have flour in a warm place.
Add eggs, one at a time with a little flour to prevent
    curdling, to creamed butter and sugar.
Add essences, curry powder, then fruit and flour alternately,
    and baking powder last.
Quickly turn mixture into a well-greased tin.
Bake in a moderate oven for 3½ hours approximately —
    180°C to begin with and after the first 45 minutes, the
    heat may be lowered.

Banana Sponge, page 37

# Christmas or Birthday Cake

450g flour
1 teaspoon baking powder
340g light brown sugar
340g butter
6 eggs
450g currants
450g raisins
450g sultanas
115g almonds
115g cherries
115g mixed peel
1 large cup milk
4 tablespoons golden syrup

Mix flour with baking powder.

Beat sugar and butter to a cream, add eggs one by one, and beat well after each egg.

Add fruit and nuts, a little at a time, and still beat well until all fruit is used.

Warm the milk and golden syrup and add.

Add the flour and baking powder.

Bake at 150°C for about 4 hours.

Keeps well.

# Ginger Ale Christmas Cake

450g currants
450g sultanas
115g cherries
450g raisins
225g peel
1 bottle ginger ale
665g butter
450g sugar
12 eggs, well beaten
675g flour
1 teaspoon cinnamon
1 nutmeg, grated
pinch of salt
115g ground almonds
2 tablespoons brandy
1 tablespoon glycerine

Cut up fruit very fine, cover with ginger ale and soak overnight.

Cream the butter and sugar, and add eggs little by little so as not to have the mixture curdle, and beat well.

Add flour and spices, fruit and almonds, then brandy and glycerine.

Cook about 3 hours at 140°C.

# Mangatainoka Christmas Cake

225g flour
¼ teaspoon grated nutmeg
¼ teaspoon baking soda
225g currants
225g raisins
225g sultanas
115g candied citron peel, cut very thin
1 teaspoon grated lemon rind
12 pitted prunes, softened in boiling water
225g butter
225g sugar
4 eggs, beaten to a stiff froth
½ cup brandy or wine
60g ground almonds
1 tablespoon icing sugar

Sift flour with nutmeg and soda. Clean and dry the fruit
(except prunes).
Cream butter and sugar. Add eggs, fruit (except prunes) and
lemon rind.
Lastly add flour, then brandy or wine. Mix thoroughly.
Put half the mixture in a prepared tin, lay on prunes, strew
with ground almonds and icing sugar. Add remainder
of mixture.
Cook at 180°C for 2½ hours.

# Wholemeal Christmas Cake

225g butter
225g raw sugar
2 eggs, beaten
½ heaped teaspoon baking soda
1 cup hot milk
2 level teaspoons curry powder
2½ breakfast cups wholemeal flour
225g sultanas
225g currants
225g raisins
60g peel
pinch of salt

Beat butter and sugar. Add eggs.

Put soda in hot milk with curry powder. (Hot milk and curry powder has the same effect as brandy and improves the flavour.)

Sift the wholemeal flour and mix with fruit.

Add salt. Add milk and flour, little by little, alternately until all is mixed in.

Bake 3 to 5 hours at 160°C for 30 minutes, then at 140°C for 1 hour, and turn to 130°C until cooked.

## Handy Hint

**Fruits, Washing Dried (Apricots, etc.) —**
Soak fruit in hot water, add 1 heaped tbsp bicarbonate of soda. Leave to soak for about 20 minutes, and then wash thoroughly in same water, working with the hands. Finally wash in clean water, and soak in the usual way.

# Crusty Cake

| | |
|---|---|
| 1 cup butter | 2 eggs, beaten |
| 2 cups flour | 1 tablespoon milk |
| 1 teaspoon baking powder | ½ cup sugar |

## Marshmallow

| | |
|---|---|
| ½ cup sugar | melted chocolate |
| 1 cup water | walnut halves to decorate |
| 2 tablespoons gelatine, melted | |

Rub butter into flour and baking powder with tips of fingers.
Add eggs, milk and sugar. Mix to a stiff dough.
Roll out very thin and bake in a moderate oven (180°C)
    until nicely brown.
When cool, spread marshmallow on top of cake,
    then chocolate.
Cut into dainty squares.
Place ½ walnut on each. (Very good.)

To make marshmallow, boil sugar and water for 15 minutes.
    (Must not be brown.)
Whip gelatine into boiled sugar and water.

# Date Sandwich Cake

1 cup dates, cut up
vanilla essence
115g butter
115g sugar
1 tablespoon golden syrup
pinch of salt
1 egg, beaten
½ cup flour
1 breakfast cup wholemeal flour
1 teaspoon baking powder

Simmer dates with 2 dessertspoons water until soft, then
beat with a fork.
Add vanilla to taste. Set aside to cool.
Cream butter and sugar. Add syrup and salt.
Add egg, flour and baking powder.
Put half the mixture in a cake tin, and spread over
date mixture.
Put on rest of cake mixture.
Bake about 30 minutes in a moderate oven (180°C).
Nice moist cake.

# Dolly Varden Cake

115g butter
½ cup sugar
4 eggs, beaten

1 teaspoon baking powder
1½ cups flour
1 cup mixed fruit

## Filling

1 tablespoon butter
225g icing sugar
juice of a good-sized lemon

Cream butter and sugar. Add eggs, baking powder and flour.
Divide mixture into three and add fruit to one.
Bake in three cake tins at 190°C for about 25 minutes.
When baked, place the three together (with fruit cake in
    middle) with the filling mixture.
Cake can also be iced on top if desired.

# Eggless Fruit Cake

1 breakfast cup sugar
1 breakfast cup cold water
2 breakfast cups mixed fruit
    (raisins, currants
    and sultanas)

115g butter
2 cups flour
1 teaspoon baking soda

Put sugar, water, fruit and butter in a saucepan, and slowly
    bring to the boil.
Simmer gently for 3 minutes. Leave to cool.
Sift flour and baking soda and add to mixture. Stir well.
Line a tin with greased paper and add mixture.
Cook in a moderate oven (180°C) for 1½ to 2 hours.
Moist, and should keep for weeks.

# Foundation Cake

85g butter
140g sugar
2 eggs

140g flour
1 teaspoon baking powder

Cream butter and sugar. Add eggs, flour and baking
powder.
Bake at 180°C for about 20 minutes.

## Plain Sponge:
Add 3 tablespoons cold milk.

## Chocolate Sponge:
Add 2 dessertspoons cocoa mixed with 3 tablespoons boiling
water.

## Orange Cake:
Add only rind of orange. Use juice for icing. Sultanas, etc.,
may also be added.

# Fruit Cake – The Best in the World

2 cups butter
2 cups light brown sugar
7 egg yolks
7 egg whites, beaten until stiff and dry
2 tablespoons milk
2 tablespoons fruit juice
450g nuts
900g currants
900g raisins
225g dates
225g peel
4 cups flour
2 teaspoons mace
2 teaspoons cinnamon
2 teaspoons baking powder
a few grains of salt

Cream butter. Add sugar gently and beat for 5 minutes.
Beat egg yolks until light and lemon coloured. Add
    egg whites.
Add to butter and sugar mixture. Add milk, fruit juice
    and nuts.
Roll fruit in flour and add. Add well-sifted dry ingredients.
Beat mixture thoroughly.
Place in a deep, round cake tin lined with several
    thicknesses of baking paper.
Bake for 4 hours or longer at 170°C.

# Fudge Cake

450g crushed wine biscuits
or any stale crushed-up
cake
225g butter

about 1 cup sugar
2 eggs, beaten
chocolate icing and nuts to
decorate

Melt butter with sugar. Add eggs.
Heat up until like honey. Add crumbs.
Press into a cake tin and leave until next day.
Ice with chocolate icing, and put some nuts on top. Walnuts
or sultanas may be added.

# Genoa Cake

225g butter
225g sugar
4 eggs
drop of lemon essence

285g flour
450g currants
225g candied peel

Cream butter and sugar. Beat in eggs and essence.
Mix together flour and fruit, then add to butter mixture.
Mix well.
Bake at 160°C for 2 hours.

# Gingerbread with Sour Milk

115g butter
6 tablespoons sugar
1 large egg
½ cup treacle
½ teaspoon baking soda
½ cup sour milk
2 cups flour
1 teaspoon ground ginger
1 teaspoon baking powder
½ teaspoon salt
1 cup raisins

Cream butter and sugar. Beat in egg, then treacle,
and mix well.
Beat soda into sour milk and add.
Stir in flour, ginger, baking powder, salt. Add raisins.
Spread on a well greased and floured shallow tin.
Bake for 20 to 30 minutes in an oven not too hot
(about 160°C).
Moist, light and fruity — sour milk keeps cake moist
without heaviness.
[Note: plain unsweetened yoghurt can be used instead
of sour milk.]

# Ginger Cake

115g butter
115g sugar
2 eggs
½ cup golden syrup,
   warmed a little
½ cup milk
2 teaspoons cinnamon
2 teaspoons ground ginger
1 teaspoon baking powder
¼ teaspoon salt

2 teaspoons mixed spice
½ teaspoon nutmeg
   (or to taste)
2 cups flour
1 teaspoon baking soda in
   ½ cup boiling water
coffee icing to decorate
pieces of preserved ginger
   cut small, to decorate

Cream butter and sugar. Add eggs, then syrup.
Add milk and all dry ingredients. Lastly, add baking soda
   in water.
Bake at 180°C for about 30 minutes.
Makes a nice ginger cake.
Ice with coffee icing and top with preserved ginger.

# Ginger Sponge with Arrowroot

3 eggs
½ cup sugar
½ cup arrowroot
1 teaspoon plain flour
1 teaspoon cream of tartar
½ teaspoon baking soda

1 teaspoon cinnamon
1 teaspoon ground ginger
1 teaspoon cocoa
1 dessertspoon golden
   syrup
cream to serve

Beat eggs for 5 minutes. Add sugar gradually, and continue
   beating until light.
Sift all other ingredients in and then add the golden syrup.
Bake in a sandwich tin in a moderate oven (180°C) for 15 to
   20 minutes.
Put together with cream.

# Gold Cake – Economical

2 cups flour
2 teaspoons baking powder
¼ teaspoon salt
½ cup butter
1 cup sugar

2 egg yolks, beaten
   until light
¾ cup milk
1 teaspoon vanilla essence

## Frosting

1 tablespoon grated
   orange rind
3 tablespoons butter
3 cups sifted sugar

2 tablespoons lemon juice
   mixed with 1 tablespoon
   water
pinch of salt

Sift flour. Add baking powder and salt. Sift twice more.
Cream butter, add sugar gradually, and cream until light.
   Add egg yolks to butter mixture.
Add flour and milk alternately. Beat after each addition
   until smooth.
Add essence and beat.
Bake in a greased pan at about 120°C to 150°C for
   50 to 60 minutes.
Use egg whites in Angel Cake (see page 33), or Meringues
   (see page 21) or Silver Cake (see page 74).

To make the frosting, add orange rind to butter and
   cream well.
Add 1 cup sugar gradually.
Add lemon and water alternately with 2 cups sugar.
   Beat until smooth.
Add salt.
Cover top and sides as well.

# Honey Date Cake

450g dates
1 teacup boiling water
1 teaspoon baking soda
225g butter
225g honey
3 eggs
255g flour, sifted
1 teaspoon grated nutmeg
¼ teaspoon salt
1 breakfast cup chopped walnuts

Pour boiling water on to dates with baking soda.
Allow to stand until nearly cold and mix with a
wooden spoon.
Beat together butter, honey and eggs.
Add flour, nutmeg, salt, dates and walnuts.
Bake in a greased tin for about 1½ hours in a moderate
oven (180°C).

# Honey Roll ~ No Butter

3 eggs
60g sugar
1 large tablespoon honey
115g flour, sifted
1 teaspoon baking powder
1 teaspoon cinnamon
2 tablespoons hot water

## Honey Filling

115g icing sugar
1 dessertspoon butter
1 dessertspoon honey
1 teaspoon lemon juice

Beat eggs and sugar well. Add honey.
Add flour, baking powder and cinnamon. Add hot water.
Bake about 10 minutes in a quick oven (220°C).
Turn out quickly on a damp cloth.
Trim off edges. Roll up in cloth and allow to stand
    2 minutes.
Unroll, and roll up without cloth. When cold, fill with the
    honey filling (or whipped cream).
To make the honey filling, beat all ingredients together.
A few chopped nuts may be added.

# Lindy Lou's Fruit Cake

115g sugar
about 1 teacup milk
450g flour
¼ teaspoon baking soda
225g butter
60g lemon peel
225g currants
225g sultanas
2 eggs
115g golden syrup, melted
almonds (if liked)

Dissolve sugar in milk. Sift flour with soda.
Rub in butter until it resembles breadcrumbs. Add peel
and fruit.
Beat eggs and add melted syrup. Add sugar and milk to this.
Combine, and beat well.
Bake in a moderate oven (180°C) for 2 hours.

## Handy Hint

**Cakes, to Post Away —**
Remove from tins to cool. Wash and sterilise tins in the oven. Line tins with fresh
paper, and pack cake just before posting. It should be out of the tin for at least
24 hours. You can pour brandy on while the cake is still hot in the tin. Fruit cakes
are good for posting.

lproof Chocolate Cake, page 43

# Log Cake

icing sugar, sifted and free of lumps
115g butter
1 egg, beaten
essence
1 tablespoon cocoa
24 malt biscuits
chopped nuts (optional)

Have sifted icing sugar ready.
Melt butter to a liquid. Add egg.
Add essence, cocoa and enough icing sugar to make a nice
spreadable consistency.
Beat well together. It is nice done in a double saucepan.
Place 4 biscuits end to end. Cover with a thin layer of icing.
Lay 4 more biscuits on top and cover again with icing, just
like bricks and mortar.
Ice all over and, if liked, sprinkle with chopped nuts.
If icing begins to harden in the bowl before it is all spread,
place the bowl in hot water for a few minutes.
Leave 2 or 3 days before cutting, and cut in thin slices.

# Louise Cake

115g butter
45g sugar
3 egg yolks, well beaten
225g flour
1 level teaspoon baking powder
raspberry jam
3 egg whites, very stiffly beaten
170g sugar
85g desiccated coconut

Cream butter and first measure of sugar. Add egg yolks.
Add flour and baking powder.
Spread in a flat tin about 26cm square. Spread with jam.
Add egg whites to second measure of sugar and coconut.
Spread on top of cake and bake for 30 minutes in a
    moderate oven (180°C).
Cut into squares while hot.

# Macaroon Cake

115g butter
115g sugar
3 egg yolks, beaten well
½ cup milk

1 teaspoon vanilla essence
170g flour, sifted
2 teaspoons baking powder
pinch of salt

## Macaroon Mixture

3 egg whites, beaten
115g sugar
1 cup coconut

Cream butter and sugar.
Add egg yolks to milk and essence, mixing well.
Add to creamed mixture. Fold in flour, baking powder
and salt.
Spread in a flat greased tin and cover top with the
macaroon mixture.
Bake at 200°C for approximately 40 minutes.

# Madeira

170g butter
170g sugar
3 eggs
225g flour

1½ teaspoons baking
powder
lemon essence

Cream butter and sugar well.
Add eggs one by one, beating well.
Sift in flour, baking powder and essence.
Bake in a moderate oven (180°C).

# Marzipan Cake

170g butter
170g caster sugar
225g flour
1 teaspoon baking powder
pinch of salt

3 eggs, beaten
½ teaspoon almond essence
strawberry jam
almond paste (see page 138)

In a warm basin, cream butter and sugar.
Sift flour, baking powder and salt — all slightly warmed,
    alternately with eggs and essence.
Bake at 180°C in 2 sandwich tins for about 30 minutes.
When cold, spread each half thinly with jam.
Stick together with a thin layer of almond paste.

# Meringue Cake

85g butter
115g caster sugar
4 egg yolks
1 tablespoon milk

1 breakfast cup flour
1 teaspoon baking powder
¼ teaspoon vanilla essence
a few grains of salt

## Meringue Mixture

4 egg whites
¾ cup sugar
115g ground almonds

Cream together butter, sugar and egg yolks.
Add other ingredients and mix.
Line a 20cm square baking tin with buttered paper.
Place mixture evenly in tin. Spread meringue mixture
    on top.
Bake for 1¼ hours at 180°C.

# Napoleon Cream Cake

2 cups cream
1 egg white, stiffly beaten
  with 1 teaspoon vanilla
2 tablespoons icing sugar

2 dessertspoons gelatine
  dissolved in 2
  tablespoons cold water
puff pastry to serve
vanilla icing to serve

Beat half the cream, not too stiffly. Add egg white.
Do not beat again but just leave on one side.
Pour other half of cream into a saucepan with icing sugar
  and gelatine.
Keep warm until gelatine is fully dissolved. If you boil this
  it will curdle.
Leave to cool.
Beat and when it starts to get thick, add the other cream
  and whip.
Turn out into a 18cm x 18cm wetted tin.
When set, place between 2 layers of puff pastry and ice with
  vanilla icing.

# Orange Cake – No Butter

3 eggs
1 cup sugar
grated rind and juice of
  1 orange

1 heaped breakfast cup flour
1 teaspoon baking powder
pinch of salt

Beat eggs with sugar for 10 minutes (all the beating need
  not be done at once).
Add orange juice and rind, and beat again.
Add flour, baking powder and salt.
Bake in a greased tin at 200°C for about 30 minutes.

# Orange Coconut Cake

115g butter
115g sugar
2 eggs, beaten
115g flour
1 teaspoon baking powder

2 tablespoons desiccated
    coconut
grated rind of 1 orange
1 tablespoon orange juice
butter icing to ice cake
    (see page 141)

Cream butter and sugar. Add eggs.
Add dry ingredients and orange rind and juice.
Bake at 190°C for about 20 minutes.
A very light and soft cake.
Ice with butter icing.

# Orange Cream Sponge

1 cup sugar
1 cup flour
2 teaspoons cream of tartar
½ teaspoon baking soda
pinch of salt
2 eggs

cream
1 teaspoon orange juice
a few drops of vanilla
    essence
a little orange peel

Sift together sugar, flour, cream of tartar, baking soda and salt.
Break eggs into a cup. Add orange juice and essence and fill
    cup to top with cream.
Beat all well together.
Grate orange peel into mixture.
Bake in sandwich tins in a moderate oven (180°C).
Make a filling of butter, icing sugar and orange juice.

# Patch Cake

225g to 285g butter
2 cups sugar
4 eggs, well beaten
3½ cups flour
3 teaspoons baking powder
1 teaspoon salt
1 cup milk
½ teaspoon nutmeg
1 teaspoon mixed spice
1 tablespoon cocoa
½ teaspoon vanilla essence
2 tablespoons golden syrup
¾ cup chopped raisins
plain butter icing, slightly flavoured with vanilla

Cream butter and sugar. Add eggs.
Sift in flour, baking powder and salt. Mix. Add milk.
Mix well and divide batter into two.
Leave one plain; add spices, cocoa, essence, syrup and
    raisins to second half.
Grease and line a square cake tin.
Put batter in, in alternate spoonfuls of each mixture.
Bake in a moderate oven (180°C) for 1½ to 2 hours.
Ice when cool.

# Pavlova Cake

4 egg whites
¾ cup caster sugar
1 teaspoon vinegar
1 teaspoon cornflour
a few drops of vanilla
essence

pinch of salt
strawberries and cream
to serve
chopped raisins soaked in
sherry or whisky to serve

Whisk eggs and sugar in a dry basin for 10 minutes with a
very strong egg whisk.
Add vinegar, then cornflour, vanilla and salt.
Beat stiff enough to stand when cut.
Line a tin with well-buttered paper (or bake in paper alone,
formed into a high-sided container).
Put into oven heated to 120°C, and turn off heat.
Leave in the oven until cold.
Cover with strawberries and cream, or raisins.

# Rainbow Cake

225g butter
1 cup sugar
4 eggs
vanilla essence
2 cups flour

2 teaspoons baking powder
1 dessertspoon cocoa
or allspice
jam

Beat butter and sugar. Add eggs, one by one.
Add vanilla, flour and baking powder.
Divide into 3 lots.
Make one pink (add a little red food colouring), one plain,
and add cocoa or allspice to the other.
Cook in 3 tins for 30 minutes at 180°C.
Stick together with jam when cool.

ise Cake, page 66

Meringue Cake, page 68

# Seed Cake

225g butter
225g sugar
3 eggs
2 heaped cups flour
½ teaspoon salt

1 large teaspoon baking powder
6 tablespoons cold water
4 teaspoons caraway seeds

Cream butter and sugar. Add eggs one by one.
Add flour to salt and baking powder.
Add half this mixture with the water.
Add rest of flour mixture and the seeds.
Bake at 180°C for about 1 hour.

# Selby Cake

115g butter
115g sugar
1 egg

200g flour
1 teaspoon baking powder
raspberry jam

Beat butter and sugar to a cream. Add egg.
Sift flour and baking powder, and add.
Grease and flour a sandwich tin.
Put in half the mixture and flatten out.
Spread with a thin layer of jam.
Cover with remaining mixture and spread evenly.
Bake in a moderate oven (180°C) for about 30 minutes.

# Ship's One Egg Fruit Cake

225g butter
½ cup sugar
1 egg
1 tablespoon golden syrup
1 tablespoon raspberry jam

1 teaspoon vinegar
2 large cups flour
450g to 675g mixed fruit
1 teaspoon baking soda
    dissolved in 1 cup milk

Cream butter and sugar. Add egg and beat.
Add golden syrup, jam and vinegar.
Add flour and fruit. Add soda and milk.
Bake slowly for 2½ hours in a moderate oven (180°C).

# Silver Cake

4 egg whites
115g butter
115g sugar
¾ cup cornflour

lemon essence
¾ cup flour
1 teaspoon baking powder
milk (if necessary)

Beat egg whites until stiff.
Cream butter and sugar.
Add egg whites and other ingredients.
Use milk to make right consistency.
Bake at 180°C for 30 minutes.

# Simnel Cake

225g butter
225g sugar
4 eggs
285g flour
1 teaspoon baking powder
60g ground rice
115g chopped mixed peel
450g currants
60g cherries

## Almond Paste

225g ground almonds
85g icing sugar
1 teaspoon almond essence
85g caster sugar
1 tablespoon melted butter
1 egg, beaten well

Cream butter and sugar. Add eggs one at a time.
Add flour, baking powder and rice, alternately with fruit.
Put half the mixture in a tin.
Cover with a layer of half the almond paste.
Add other half cake mixture.
Bake cake in a moderate oven (180°C) for about 2½ hours.
When cooked decorate with other half almond paste
mixture. (Almond paste may be bought readymade.)

# Snow Cake ~ Uncooked

2 tablespoons sugar
½ breakfast cup cold water
1 tablespoon gelatine
½ breakfast cup boiling water
2 egg whites
a little vanilla essence

Boil sugar and cold water for a minute or two.
Dissolve gelatine in the boiling water.
Combine the two, and when a little cooler, stir in unbeaten
    egg whites and vanilla.
When cool, and just beginning to set, whip up until foamy
    and thick.
Line a sandwich tin with wet baking paper.
Pour in mixture.
Sets very quickly. Delicious spread with whipped cream
    and passionfruit.

# Spiced Crumbly Top Cake

2 cups flour
2 teaspoons baking powder
½ teaspoon salt
½ teaspoon nutmeg
¼ teaspoon cinnamon
¾ cup sugar
60g butter
2 eggs, unbeaten
⅔ cup milk

## Crumble Mixture

60g butter
1 cup brown sugar
4 tablespoons flour
½ teaspoon cinnamon
⅛ teaspoon salt

Sift flour, baking powder, salt, nutmeg and cinnamon.
Add sugar. Rub in butter.
Add eggs. Mix well.
Add milk and stir until smooth.
Pour into a square tin and sprinkle with the
    crumble mixture.
To make the crumble mixture, blend all ingredients with a
    fork. (Half a cup of chopped walnuts is very nice too.)
Bake in a moderate oven (180°C) for 30 to 45 minutes.

# Sponge – Cold Oven

3 eggs
1 teacup sugar
1 breakfast cup flour
1 teaspoon cream of tartar

1 tablespoon butter
2 tablespoons milk
½ teaspoon baking soda

Do not turn oven on until sponge is ready to be put in.
Beat eggs and sugar well. Mix in flour and cream of tartar.
Dissolve butter and milk in a saucepan. Add baking soda.
Mix all well together.
Put mixture into two sandwich tins and put in the oven.
Bake at 190°C for 25 to 30 minutes.


# Sponge – Easy

3 egg whites, beaten
    until stiff
1 breakfast cup sugar
3 egg yolks, unbeaten
1 cup flour, sifted

1 teaspoon baking powder
a walnut-sized piece
    of butter
¼ cup boiling water

Fold egg whites into sugar. Let stand for 10 minutes
    to dissolve.
Drop in unbeaten egg yolks and beat well.
Fold in flour and baking powder.
Add butter dissolved in the boiling water.
Bake in a slow oven (120°C) for 30 minutes.

# Vienna Cake – 2 Eggs

1½ tablespoons cocoa
about ¾ cup boiling water
1½ tablespoons
    raspberry jam
115g butter
170g sugar
2 eggs

vanilla essence
225g flour
2 teaspoons baking powder
pinch of salt
chocolate icing (see
    page 141)

Make cocoa to a thin paste with a little of the boiling water.
    Stir in the jam.
Make up to ¾ cup with boiling water. Let it cool.
Cream butter and sugar. Add eggs one by one, beating well.
    Add vanilla essence.
Sift flour, baking powder and salt very well. Add alternately
    with the liquid.
Bake in a flat tin in a moderate oven (180°C) for
    approximately 45 minutes.
Ice with chocolate icing. Mark with a fork.

# Walnut Cake

115g butter
170g sugar
3 eggs
60g crushed walnuts
1 teaspoon mixed spice

1 teaspoon baking powder
170g flour
2 tablespoons warm milk
icing
walnuts

Cream butter and sugar. Add eggs one by one.
In a separate bowl, mix walnuts, spice, baking powder and
    flour together.
Add milk alternately with mixed dry ingredients.
Bake at 180°C for 30 minutes.
Ice and put walnuts on icing.

# Wedding Cake — Three-tiered

565g butter
565g sugar
12 to 14 eggs, depending on size, well whipped
675g flour
2 large teaspoons baking powder (or 1 teaspoon
    each cream of tartar and baking soda)
pinch of salt
15g mixed spice
450g raisins
225g dates
450g currants
450g sultanas
225g candied cherries
115g mixed peel
115g almonds
1 teaspoon lemon essence
a few drops of almond essence
2 tablespoons brandy

## Almond Icing

1.8kg icing sugar
4 egg whites, beaten stiff
674g ground almonds
a little almond essence

## Royal Icing

4 egg whites, beaten stiff
enough icing sugar to make icing stiff and to spread nicely
    and force through icing tubes
lemon essence

Work butter and sugar until creamy.

Add eggs, alternately with flour sifted with baking powder, salt and spices.

Clean and chop fruit, but not too finely, and add with nuts and essences.

Add brandy and mix thoroughly.

Place mixture in a 30cm diameter, 10cm deep tin lined with several layers of white paper.

Bake 6 to 7 hours in a moderate oven (180°C).

Prepare the same mixture again and put two-thirds in a 25cm diameter tin.

Put remaining mixture in a 20cm diameter tin.

Bake for 4 hours or longer.

Make the large tier one day and the 2 smaller ones the next day, as few home owners would have an oven to hold 3 tins at a time.

Do not open oven until large cake has been cooking for 2 hours.

Ice with almond icing then royal icing.

Note: If almond icing is too stiff, add an egg yolk beaten in. If not stiff enough, add more icing sugar.

# Wedding or Festival Cake

675g sultanas
675g currants
450g raisins
225g mixed peel
115g preserved ginger
115g preserved cherries, if
   desired (for colour,
   not flavour)
1 teaspoon grated mixed
   orange and lemon rind
450g butter beaten with 1
   teaspoon glycerine
340g light brown sugar

8 eggs
570g flour
1 level teaspoon baking
   powder
light sprinkling of cayenne
   pepper (to bring out
   flavour — no spirits
   needed)
1 teaspoon ground ginger
1 teaspoon nutmeg
1 teaspoon vanilla essence
1 teaspoon almond essence

After mixing the fruit together, make it hot in the oven.

Cream butter and sugar, then beat in eggs, adding one
   by one.

Mix together the flour, baking powder and spices. Stir into
   the creamed mixture.

Fold in the fruit and essences. Mix well.

Grease a 28cm tin and line with paper. Place cake batter in
   the tin.

After scraping the bowl, mix that batter from sides of the
   bowl well into cake mixture in the tin.

Make a fair-sized hole in the centre of the cake with your
   hand so it will rise evenly as it cooks.

Cook at 150°C for 5 to 6 hours, according to depth of cake.

nnel Cake, page 75

Bran & Date Muffins, page 87

# Wholemeal One Egg Chocolate Sponge

| | |
|---|---|
| 115g butter | salt |
| 1 cup brown sugar | 2 tablespoons cocoa |
| ½ teaspoon baking soda dissolved in ½ cup milk | 1 teaspoon baking powder |
| | 1 cup flour |
| 1 egg | vanilla essence |
| ½ cup wholemeal flour | ¼ cup hot water |

Cream butter and sugar.
Add baking soda and milk, and egg.
Add remaining ingredients, with vanilla last.
Add hot water.
Bake in a moderate oven (180°C) for 30 minutes.

# Wholemeal Family Cake

| | |
|---|---|
| 1½ cups milk | 3 cups wholemeal flour |
| 225g sugar | 1 tablespoon cocoa |
| 115g butter | 1½ teaspoons cinnamon |
| 3 tablespoons golden syrup | 2 cups nuts |
| 1½ teaspoons baking soda | 1 cup dates |
| ½ cup white flour | |

Stir 1 cup milk in a saucepan with sugar, butter and golden
    syrup, until butter melts.
Dissolve soda in the other ½ cup milk.
Mix the dry ingredients, and add the warm mixture and
    nuts and dates.
Add the soda last.
Bake at 180°C for 30 minutes and allow to cool before
    turning out.

# Wonder Sponge Cake

1 cup flour
2 teaspoons baking powder
1 cup sugar

2 level teaspoons butter
2 eggs
a little milk

Sift flour with baking powder, and mix with sugar in a
  basin. Make a well in the centre.
Melt butter in cup. Drop in eggs with butter in the cup, and
  fill cup up with milk.
Pour into flour and beat for 5 minutes.
Bake in a moderate oven (180°C) for 8 to 10 minutes.

# Yankee Doodle Cake

½ cup butter
1 cup sugar
2 eggs, well beaten
1½ cups flour
1 cup minced raisins
½ teaspoon baking soda
  dissolved in ½ cup milk

cream filling (or knob of
  butter, icing sugar, vanilla
  and chopped walnuts)
icing and nuts to decorate
rum essence (or real rum)
  (optional)

Beat butter and sugar. Add eggs.
Add flour, raisins and then baking soda and milk.
Mix raisins in well.
Cook in 2 sandwich tins in a moderate oven (180°C) for
  about 30 minutes.
Join with cream filling, or make a rich filling by dissolving
  butter in a little boiling water and adding icing sugar,
  vanilla and chopped walnuts.
Ice top and decorate with nuts. A little rum essence (or real
  rum) can be added to the raisins — they sink to the
  bottom when cooking.

# Breads, Scones & Teacakes

# Australian Cheese Drop Scones

2 cups flour, sifted
2 teaspoons baking powder
1½ teaspoons salt

60g to 85g butter
¾ cup milk
1 cup grated cheese

Sift together flour, baking powder and salt.
Melt butter in a cup and fill cup with milk. Pour into flour.
Add cheese.
Mix lightly into a nice dough, until all liquid is used.
Stir vigorously until dough is nice and soft. The bowl should
now be clean.
Drop from a teaspoon or dessertspoon onto an ungreased
baking sheet.
Bake in a hot oven (220°C) for 10 to 15 minutes.
Makes about 18 to 20 scones.
Nice for supper.


# Belgian Bun

115g butter
115g sugar
225g flour
1 teaspoon baking powder
1 egg, well beaten

a little milk
lemon cheese (see page 146)
blanched almonds to
    decorate

Cream butter and sugar. Add flour and baking powder.
Make into a fairly stiff dough with egg and milk.
Divide into two parts.
Press each with fingers into a round shape.
Place one half in a pie plate or dish, spread with lemon cheese.
Put other round on top. Decorate with blanched almonds.
Bake in a moderate oven (180°C) for 15 to 20 minutes.

# Berkshire Crumpets

15g compressed yeast  
a little sugar  
450g flour  
½ teaspoon salt  
1 egg, beaten  
1 cup milk and tepid water

Stir yeast to a cream with sugar.  
Sift flour and salt into a warm basin.  
Stir egg into yeast with milk. Pour into flour.  
Beat well until smooth, adding more milk or water until a
smooth batter, slightly thicker than pancake mix.  
Cover and leave in a warm place for 1½ hours.  
Put muffin tins on a hot griddle.  
Half fill with batter and cook, turning once only.  
Serve toasted and buttered.  
Condensed milk tins or similar can be used cut down for
muffin rings.

# Bran & Date Muffins

1 cup dates, cut up coarsely
(could use raisins or
sultanas)  
1 cup white or wholemeal
flour  
1 cup bran  
3 level teaspoons baking
powder  
½ teaspoon salt  
2 teaspoons sugar  
1 egg, beaten well  
1 cup milk  
2 tablespoons melted butter

Add dates (or sultanas) to dry sifted ingredients.  
Mix egg, milk and butter.  
Pour at once into dry ingredients, and mix just enough to
blend. Do not beat.  
Grease small muffin pans and fill to two-thirds full.  
Bake at 200°C for approximately 20 minutes.

# Bread

10 cups flour (3 wholemeal and 7 white is a good light loaf)
1 level tablespoon salt
2 teaspoons compressed yeast
2 tablespoons sugar
3½ to 4 cups warm water
melted butter

Sift flour and salt into a warmed bowl.

In another basin, work yeast and sugar together until liquid. Add warm water.

Pour yeast mixture into middle of flour and gradually work in flour from the sides until a light dough (slightly moister than scone dough).

Cover with a clean cloth, then a rug or blanket — it must not cool too quickly.

Put in a warm place overnight.

Next day, turn out on a floured board and sprinkle with flour.

Knead with back of fingers, folding in as much air as possible. Knead for at least 15 minutes.

Shape into loaves and put in greased tins to half full.

Stand in a warm place for 1 hour, or until it rises to double the size.

Bake for about 1 hour at 200°C.

Do not open oven for first 45 minutes.

Brush over top with melted butter.

Gingerbread - No Eggs, page 91

# Brown Health Loaf

2 large cups wholemeal flour
2 teaspoons baking powder
½ teaspoon salt
1 tablespoon butter
1 cup chopped dates, raisins
    and nuts

1 dessertspoon golden
    syrup dissolved in 1 cup
    hot water
½ cup cold milk

Mix wholemeal flour, baking powder and salt. Rub in
    butter.
Add dates, raisins and nuts.
Mix golden syrup and water with milk.
Mix with dry ingredients.
Bake in a greased tin for about 1¼ hours in a moderate
    oven (180°C).

# Cheese Muffins

1 egg, beaten lightly
¼ teaspoon salt
¾ cup milk
1½ cups flour
2 teaspoons baking powder

½ cup finely grated or finely
    sliced cheese
extra beaten egg to brush
    muffins

Mix egg with salt and milk.
Sift flour and baking powder, and add cheese.
Make into a dough with the liquid, mixing well.
Roll out, cut into rounds. Brush with beaten egg.
Bake for 10 minutes in a fairly hot oven (200°C), or cook in
    patty tins.
Delicious split, spread with butter, and eaten hot.

# Cinnamon Tea Cake

1 teaspoon salt
450g flour
2 teaspoons baking powder
3 tablespoons butter
1 egg, beaten

2 cups milk
vanilla or lemon essence
cinnamon
sugar
melted butter or cream

Mix first three ingredients. Rub in butter.
Add beaten egg, milk and vanilla.
Mix to a soft dough.
Roll out to 20mm thick.
Place in a shallow dish and cover with a mixture of
    cinnamon, sugar and melted butter or cream.
Bake in a quick oven (200°C) for about 15 minutes.
May be served hot or cold.

# Date Bread

1 cup chopped dates
1 level teaspoon baking soda
¾ cup boiling water
1 egg, beaten
½ cup sugar

pinch of salt
1 teaspoon vanilla essence
1½ breakfast cups flour
1 large teaspoon baking
    powder

Put dates in a basin with the baking soda.
Pour boiling water over and stand to cool.
Mix egg with sugar, salt and vanilla in a basin.
    Add date mixture.
Stir in flour and baking powder.
Bake in a well-greased tin for about 1¼ hours, or less,
    depending on size.
To have bread smooth and glossy, cover with paper
    while baking.

# Date & Raisin Loaf

1 cup dates
1 cup raisins or sultanas
½ cup sugar
½ cup nuts (optional)
60g butter

1½ cups hot water
2 breakfast cups flour
2 level teaspoons baking
soda

Put dates, raisins, sugar, nuts, butter and hot water in a
saucepan and boil for 8 to 10 minutes.
Allow to cool then add flour and baking soda.
Mix all together in a shallow tin and bake fairly slowly
(160°C) for 45 minutes.
This is a moist loaf and keeps well. Improved by using
wholemeal flour.

# Gingerbread ~ No Eggs

½ cup sugar
1 level tablespoon ginger
2 cups flour
¼ cup or 4 tablespoons
butter, melted

½ cup treacle
1 teaspoon baking soda
dissolved in a little hot
water
½ cup milk

Put all dry ingredients into a basin.
Melt butter and treacle together.
Mix baking soda, butter and treacle with dry ingredients.
Beat in milk.
Bake at 180°C for 1½ hours.
This keeps beautifully moist.

# Gingerbread – 2 Eggs

2 tablespoons butter
1 breakfast cup brown sugar
2 teaspoons ground ginger
2 teaspoons cinnamon
2 tablespoons golden syrup
2 eggs, beaten

2 breakfast cups flour
2 level teaspoons baking
   soda dissolved in
   warm water
1 breakfast cup milk

## Icing

225g brown sugar
4 tablespoons cream

30g butter
vanilla to taste

Cream butter and sugar.
Add ginger, cinnamon, syrup and beaten eggs.
Add flour, baking soda and milk.
Bake at 180°C for 30 minutes.
To make the icing, boil all ingredients together until it thickens.


# Girdle Scones

2 heaped teacups flour
½ teaspoon salt

3 teaspoons baking powder
milk and water to mix

Mix all together into a soft dough. Do not have dough
   too stiff.
Roll out and cut into quarters.
Take each section in right hand, turn over on to left hand,
   and slip onto girdle. Thus the underneath floury side
   is on top.
Lightly brush off flour from what is now the top, and turn
   when brown. This helps to stop toughness.
Stand them on edge for a few minutes when cooked.

# Griddle Pancakes

1¼ cups flour
1 teaspoon baking powder
½ teaspoon salt
1 teaspoon sugar
1 cup milk
2 egg yolks, slightly beaten
2 tablespoons melted butter
2 egg whites, beaten
quince or other jelly, or bacon or sausage to serve

Sift flour, baking powder, salt and sugar twice.
Mix milk and egg yolks.
Add flour gradually and mix to a smooth batter.
Add butter. Fold in egg whites.
Bake on a hot greased griddle.
Spread with jelly and roll, or roll around bacon or sausage.

# Hot Cross Buns

450g flour
pinch of salt
1 teaspoon mixed spice
60g butter
60g mixed candied peel
60g sultanas
60g currants
1 level teaspoon powdered cinnamon
2 tablespoons caster sugar
22g compressed yeast
1 cup lukewarm milk
1 egg

Sift flour with salt and spice.

Rub in butter and add prepared fruit, cinnamon and sugar
(keep back half the sugar to mix with yeast).

Mix sugar and yeast until liquid. Stir in milk.

Strain liquid into centre of dry ingredients.

Make into a soft dough, adding the egg.

Divide into small portions, shape into buns, and put on a
greased oven tray.

Mark with a cross. Leave to rise until twice the size.

Bake in a hot oven (200°C) for 20 minutes.

Brush over with sugar and milk. Return to oven for
2 minutes.

# Mary's Bread

6 cups wholemeal flour
2 teaspoons salt
2 teaspoons dried yeast
2½ to 3 cups milk at blood heat
2 teaspoons honey

Sift wholemeal flour and salt.
Mix yeast with milk and honey. Make sure it is well
dissolved.
Add to flour and salt.
Mix into a scone consistency and turn out.
Knead a little and replace in basin.
Leave in a warm place for 2 hours, or until it doubles in size.
Turn out and knead well.
Form into loaves and leave again for 45 minutes to 1 hour in
a warm place.
Bake in a moderate oven (180°C) for 45 minutes to 1 hour.

# Handy Hint

**Bread, to Freshen —**

1.  Put bread in a brown paper bag. Put into a hot oven for 30 minutes or
    more, depending on the size of the loaf. A large loaf takes about 1 hour.
2.  Or stand a pie dish of boiling water on one rung of the oven. On
    rack directly above, put the loaf so that it gets the steam. Have oven
    at 180°C, top off, bottom on low. Leave 20 minutes.

# Muffins

2 tablespoons sugar
30g yeast dissolved in a little lukewarm water
900g flour
15g salt
2 cups milk, or milk and water
rice flour

Add sugar to yeast. Sift flour with salt.
Put milk in a basin and add a little of the flour.
Pour in yeast and sugar, and work together.
Work in remainder of flour, and knead well.
Leave to rise in a warm place for 1 hour. Then knead dough
    and divide as required.
Round each piece carefully, and leave in a warm place to
    rise, about 1 hour or more.
Dust each piece with rice flour, if available.
When double in size, roll out with a rolling pin to about
    25mm thick, still keeping the round shape.
Bake on an ungreased hot plate, but not too hot, or muffins
    will be doughy in centre.
As they bake, turn each over with a broad knife.
When brown on both sides, reduce heat until thoroughly
    cooked.
Two tablespoons of butter may be added to the mixture,
    if liked.

Cross Buns, page 94

Pikelets, page 97

# Nut & Raisin Loaf

3 cups plain flour
(or 2 cups plain and
1 cup wholemeal)
3 teaspoons baking powder
1 cup sugar
1 teaspoon salt

1 teaspoon ground
cinnamon
1 egg, beaten
1½ cups milk
1 cup raisins
1 cup chopped walnuts

Sift dry ingredients. Add egg and milk, stir in and mix well.
Add raisins and nuts.
Pour into a greased tin. Let stand for 30 minutes.
Bake in a moderate oven (180°C) for about 1½ hours.

# Pikelets

1 cup flour
1 tablespoon sugar
½ teaspoon salt
1 teaspoon cream of tartar

½ teaspoon baking soda
1 egg
milk to mix to stiff paste
1 teaspoon melted butter

Put all dry ingredients in a bowl.
Break in egg and mix in milk. Add butter.
Mix well and let stand for 30 minutes.
Drop in spoonful lots on hot girdle.

# Pikelets ~ without Butter

1 breakfast cup flour
2 level teaspoons cream
of tartar
pinch of salt

1 level teaspoon baking
soda
2 level tablespoons sugar
1 egg
¾ cup milk

Sift flour, cream of tartar, salt and baking soda into a basin.
Add sugar.
Make a well in centre of flour, and break in the egg.
Add milk and mix well.
Cook on hot greased girdle.
Place on towel and keep covered to make them nice
and soft.

# Potato & Cheese Gems

2 dessertspoons butter
pinch of salt
1 cup milk

2 eggs, beaten
3 cups mashed potatoes
¾ cup grated cheese

Dissolve butter and salt in milk. Add eggs.
Mix with potato and cheese, stirring slowly to mix.
Drop in buttered, very hot gem irons, sprinkle with flour
and cook until brown on top.
Split and butter, and eat hot.

# Raisin Cheese Scones

2 cups flour
2 teaspoons baking powder
½ teaspoon salt
½ cup raisins

8 tablespoons grated cheese
3 tablespoons butter
1 cup milk

Sift flour, baking powder and salt together.
Add raisins and cheese. Cut in the butter.
Add milk and mix.
Roll out lightly, shape into biscuits.
Bake in a hot oven (220°C) until brown, about 15 minutes.
These should be eaten hot.

# Sally Lunns – with Baking Powder

2 breakfast cups flour, sifted
2 teaspoons baking powder
good pinch of salt
½ cup soft sugar
1 tablespoon butter

¾ cup milk
1 egg
½ teaspoon lemon essence
slices of candied peel

Mix all dry ingredients together. Rub butter in well.
Add milk, beaten with egg and essence.
Pat on a board until 12mm thick.
Cut into diamond-shaped cakes.
Glaze each with milk and sugar, or with egg.
Place 1 piece candied peel on top of each cake.
Bake until well browned in a hot oven (220°C).

# Sally Lunns – Real

30g compressed yeast
2 cups milk, scalded and cooled to lukewarm
30g sugar
2 eggs, beaten well
½ teaspoon salt
60g butter
675g flour
white sugar for sprinkling

Dissolve yeast in a portion of the milk and add sugar.
Add salt to eggs.
Cream butter well and just melt it.
Mix all together well with flour — add yeast last.
Beat until smooth.
Pour into well-greased shallow pans, or muffin rings on a
    baking sheet.
Half fill rings, then cover and allow to rise in a warm place
    for about 1 hour, until nearly full.
Just before baking, sprinkle tops with granulated sugar.
Bake in a good oven (180°C) for about 20 minutes.
Condensed milk tins, or similar tins, may be cut down for
    muffin rings.

# Scones

225g flour
½ teaspoon salt
4 level teaspoons baking powder
2 tablespoons butter
⅔ cup milk

Sift flour, salt and baking powder together.
Rub in butter until like crumbs.
Make a well, and pour in milk.
Mix quickly with a knife or spatula.
Knead very lightly for about half a minute.
Pat or roll lightly to 12mm.
Cut with floured knife or cutter.
Place on ungreased, unfloured oven tray.
Bake in hot oven at 220°C for about 10 minutes, until
    golden brown.

# Wholemeal Scones – Never Fail

Chief points for success: Quite a moist mixture, plenty of rising, quick working, and a hot oven.

> 2 heaped cups wholemeal flour
> 2 large heaped teaspoons baking powder
> ½ large teaspoon salt
> 30g to 60g melted butter (quite liquid)
> about 1 cup milk
> 1 dessertspoon brown sugar (optional)

Mix dry ingredients.

Fill the cup containing the butter with milk.

Mix into dry ingredients very quickly, making a soft dough.

Turn onto a board, press quickly with palm of hand to about 6mm thick.

Cut in squares. Flour slightly and shake flour off.

Cook in hot oven (220°C) for about 15 minutes.

If liked, mix in 1 dessertspoon brown sugar with butter.

Turn oven down a little if browning too fast.

# Sugar Top Buns

½ cup sugar
½ cup butter
1 cup water
2 cups flour
2 teaspoons baking powder
½ cup sultanas
1 egg, well beaten
few drops of lemon essence

Boil sugar, butter and water. Set aside to cool.

Sift flour and baking powder in a basin. Add sultanas.

Mix all to a soft dough with the liquid. Add egg and essence.

Put dessertspoonfuls onto a greased oven tray. Sprinkle tops with sugar.

Bake at 180°C for about 15 minutes.

They should rise and crack, and be beautifully light. The secret is to have the dough very light.

# Vienna Rolls

900g flour
60g butter
1 teaspoon salt
1 tablespoon compressed
   yeast

15g sugar
2 cups lukewarm milk
2 eggs, beaten

Put flour in a warm basin. Rub in butter and add salt.
Put yeast in a cup with sugar, and work until smooth
   and liquid.
Add half the milk and leave in a warm place for about
   10 minutes.
Mix eggs with remainder of milk. Add to yeast mixture.
Put into flour, mixing well.
Knead to a light dough. Leave in a warm place for 1 hour.
Knead and divide into 12 pieces. Knead each to form into a roll.
Place on baking tin in a warm place for about 1 hour.
Bake in a quick oven (220°C) for about 20 minutes.
When baked, brush over with beaten egg straight away.

# Virginian Short'nin' Bread

2 cups flour
½ cup light brown sugar
225g butter

Mix flour and sugar.
Rub in butter.
Put on a floured board and pat to 12mm thickness.
Cut into shapes.
Bake in a moderate oven at 170°C to 180°C for
   20 to 25 minutes.

Scones, page 101

## Waffles (1)

2 cups flour
¼ cup cornflour
4 teaspoons baking powder
½ teaspoon salt
2 eggs, beaten well

2 cups milk
4 tablespoons melted butter
butter and maple syrup
    to serve

Beat dry ingredients into eggs and milk.
Add butter and beat well with an egg beater.
Bake in hot waffle irons.
Recipe may be halved.
Serve hot with butter and maple syrup.

## Waffles (2)

2 cups flour
3 tablespoons baking
    powder
½ teaspoon salt

2 egg yolks, beaten slightly
1¾ cups milk
4 tablespoons melted butter
2 egg whites, beaten stiff

Sift flour, baking powder and salt.
Mix egg yolks with milk. Add to dry ingredients and beat
    thoroughly.
Add butter and stir well. Fold in egg whites.
Bake in hot waffle irons.

# White Bread

4 dessertspoons sweetened
   condensed milk
2½ cups tepid water
40g dried yeast

1 cup flour
6 cups flour, sifted
1 slightly rounded
   dessertspoon salt

Pour condensed milk into a basin and add water. Stir until
   thoroughly blended.

Add yeast and beat until slightly frothy.

Add 1 cup flour and fold in.

Lightly cover, and leave in a warm place to work for about
   15 minutes.

Put 6 cups sifted flour and the salt in a large basin.

When yeast is frothy, and has a scum on top, combine with
   flour and salt.

Mix to a good stiff dough using a knife.

Remove from basin and knead well on a floured board.

Dust inside basin with flour and place kneaded dough back
   in and cover.

Let rise again for 45 minutes. The dough should be half its
   size again.

Take out and knead again.

Pat out to a 25mm thickness and cut into quarters.

Shape up and place 2 pieces in each of 2 bread tins.

Cover and allow to rise until dough is about 18mm from top
   of tins.

Place in oven at 230°C for 3 to 4 minutes.

Lower oven to 180°C and bake another 45 minutes.

After 8 minutes' baking, look at it and lower oven
   temperature if necessary.

# Wholemeal Bread ~ No Kneading

8 breakfast cups wholemeal flour
1 teaspoon salt
40g dried yeast
about 3½ cups warm water
1 teaspoon raw or brown sugar
1 tablespoon malt (if liked)

Mix flour and salt. Dissolve yeast in water with sugar (and malt if using).

Pour into flour, and stir and knead for 5 minutes. If not the right consistency, add flour or water accordingly.

Mould into loaves and put in greased tins.

Cover and put in a warm place (oven slightly heated) until double in size, about 1½ hours.

Bake about 30 minutes at 220°C to 230°C.

When baked, take loaves from tins and return to oven for a few minutes to crisp up.

# Wholemeal Bread ~ No Yeast

| | |
|---|---|
| 1 tablespoon golden syrup or treacle | 2 cups wholemeal flour |
| | ¼ teaspoon salt |
| 1 cup milk | 4 teaspoons baking powder |

Melt syrup in milk.

Mix flour, salt and baking powder. Stir into syrup and milk quickly.

Let mixture stand for a short while to rise.

Put in a greased tin and bake about 45 minutes in a moderate oven (180°C).

A nice moist loaf.


# Wholemeal Loaf

| | |
|---|---|
| 1 tablespoon golden syrup | 1 dessertspoon salt |
| ½ cake compressed yeast | 1½ breakfast cups milk (or |
| 3 breakfast cups wholemeal flour | milk and water), warmed to blood heat |

Mix syrup and yeast on a saucer.

Sift flour and salt. Make a well in flour.

Pour in yeast and syrup mixture.

Add milk, beating all the time and working in the yeast.

Continue to beat when all milk is in for 3 or 4 minutes.

> A fairly moist mixture is needed for this bread, so that if more milk is needed, heat to blood temperature as before.

Let rise in a greased tin for 1 hour.

Bake for about 1 hour in a fairly hot oven.

No kneading required.

# Yule Bread

| | |
|---|---|
| 45g compressed yeast | 3 or 4 eggs, beaten |
| warm milk to mix | 450g currants |
| 900g flour | 225g sultanas |
| 2 teaspoons salt | 115g mixed peel |
| 340g butter | 1 teaspoon cinnamon |
| 340g sugar | ½ small nutmeg, grated |

Crumble yeast into a little lukewarm milk with a pinch of
sugar and let rise.

Warm flour in basin, add salt and rub in butter. Add sugar.

Pour yeast into centre, mix and let rise for 15 minutes.

Stir in eggs, and as much warm milk as will make a
light dough.

Beat well and leave to rise about 1 hour.

Add fruit, cinnamon, nutmeg, and let rise another hour.

Put in tins lined with paper and let rise again.

Bake in moderate oven (180°C), time according to size
of loaf.

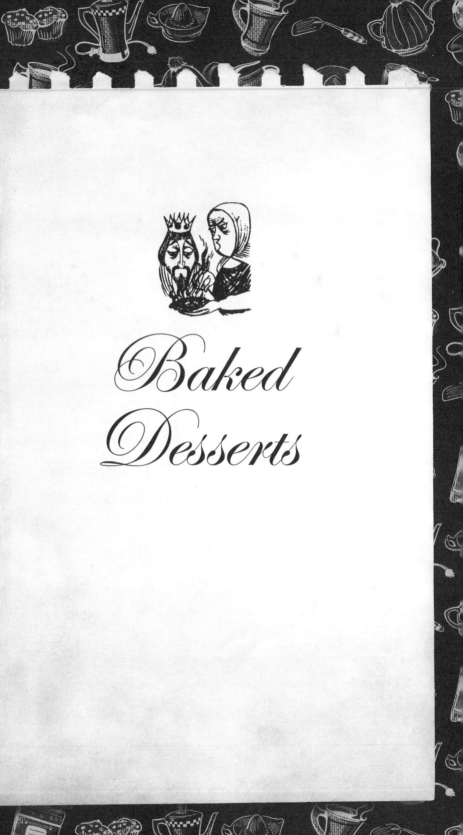

# Baked Desserts

# Apple Brown Betty

| | |
|---|---|
| 2 cups fine breadcrumbs | ½ cup sugar or honey |
| 2 tablespoons melted butter or fat | cinnamon or other spices |
| 2 cups sliced apples or other fruit | grated rind of 1 lemon or orange |
| | ½ cup fruit juice or water |

Mix breadcrumbs with butter.

Arrange layers of buttered crumbs and apple slices in pudding dish.

Sprinkle each layer of fruit with sugar, cinnamon and lemon rind.

Finish with a layer of crumbs.

Pour juice or water over top. Bake at 180°C for 45 minutes approximately.

# Apple Crisp

| | |
|---|---|
| 4 apples, peeled and sliced | 2½ tablespoons butter |
| ¾ cup cold water | ¾ cup flour |
| cinnamon | ½ cup sugar |

Arrange apples in pie dish and pour over cold water and sprinkle with cinnamon.

Rub butter into flour and sugar until crumbly, and sprinkle on top of apples.

Bake for 30 minutes.

No sugar is added to the apple as it soaks through from the top.

# Apple Dumplings

900g cooking apples, peeled and quartered
3 cups sugar
1 cup hot water

## Batter

⅓ cup butter
⅓ cup sugar
1 egg, beaten
2¼ cups flour
2¼ teaspoons baking powder
¾ teaspoon salt
1⅛ cups milk
cinnamon

Add apples to a syrup made with sugar and hot water.
Simmer until soft but unbroken.
Cream butter, add sugar gradually, then add egg.
Sift flour, baking powder and salt, adding alternately with
the milk.
Butter a good pie dish and drop in spoonfuls of batter,
alternately with spoonfuls of hot apples and syrup.
Pour remaining hot syrup over. Sprinkle with cinnamon and
bake in a hot oven (220°C) for 30 minutes.
Delicious with crisp brown bits of pastry risen through little
rivers of syrup.

Blackberry Cobbler, page 116

# Apple Dumplings Baked in Syrup

2 cups flour
2 teaspoons baking powder
1 teaspoon salt
¾ cup butter
½ cup milk
apples, peeled and cored

sugar
cinnamon
nutmeg
dates for stuffing (if liked)
custard to serve

## Syrup

1 cup sugar
1 cup water
2 tablespoons butter

¼ teaspoon ground
cinnamon
¼ teaspoon ground nutmeg

Sift flour, baking powder and salt.
Cut in the butter. Add milk and mix.
Roll out to 6mm thick and cut into squares.
Place an apple in centre of each, sprinkle with sugar,
cinnamon and nutmeg.
If liked, stuff with dates.
Gather corners of the pastry, pinch together and put in a
baking dish.
To make the syrup, boil ingredients for 5 minutes.
Pour over dumplings and bake for 30 to 40 minutes in a
moderate oven (180°C).
Serve with custard.

# Apple Ginger Upside-Down Cake

3 or 4 apples, thickly sliced
2 teaspoons cinnamon
⅓ cup sugar
½ cup butter
½ cup boiling water
1 cup golden syrup
2½ cups flour
2 teaspoons ground ginger
1 teaspoon baking soda
½ teaspoon salt
cream or custard to serve

Put apples in a buttered dish. Sprinkle with cinnamon
and sugar.
Melt butter in the boiling water. Add golden syrup.
Sift in the flour, ginger, baking soda and salt.
Pour on top of apples.
Bake for about 45 minutes in a moderate oven (180°C).
Turn out upside down.
Serve with cream or custard.

# Baked Rolypoly

225g flour
115g butter
2 teaspoons baking powder

pinch of salt
apricot jam

## Syrup

½ cup sugar
60g butter
1½ cups water

Make first 4 ingredients into a paste.
Roll out and spread with apricot jam. Roll up.
Put in a baking dish and pour over syrup.
To make the syrup, bring ingredients to the boil, pour over
the pudding.
Bake for 1½ hours in a moderate oven (180°C).

# Beverly Hills Butterscotch Pie

2 heaped teaspoons butter
1 cup brown sugar
2 tablespoons flour
2 egg yolks

1 cup milk
1 baked pie shell
2 egg whites
4 tablespoons sugar

Cream butter, 1 cup of sugar and flour together.
Mix egg yolks with milk, and bring to boiling point.
Remove from heat, pour over first mixture, and cook
until thick.
Pour into pie crust.
Beat egg whites to meringues with 4 tablespoons sugar.
Put on top of pie and brown in oven.

# Blackberry Cobbler

3 cups blackberries
1 cup water
juice of 1 lemon
sugar to taste
2 tablespoons sugar

2 tablespoons flour
dab of butter
1 sheet short pastry (or
    crushed biscuits or
    sponge cake crumbs)

Cook blackberries in the water with lemon juice and sugar.
When cold, put into a pie dish.
Sprinkle with sugar and flour and dab of butter.
Cover with a good sheet of pastry or crushed biscuits or
    sponge cake crumbs, and dab with butter.
Cook in a good oven (180°C) for 20 to 30 minutes.

# Blackberry Surprise

enough blackberries to
    almost fill a pie dish
60g butter
60g sugar

115g flour
½ teaspoon baking powder
cream or custard to serve

If blackberries are seedy, it is nicer to pour through a sieve
    after they are cooked.
Mix dry ingredients well. Rub butter in until mixture
    resembles breadcrumbs.
Sprinkle evenly over top of hot fruit.
Bake at 190°C for 30 minutes until a nice light brown.
Serve with cream or custard.

# Boston Chocolate Pudding

This sounds queer but works out beautifully.

| | |
|---|---|
| 1 cup flour | 2 tablespoons melted butter |
| ¼ cup sugar | 1 teaspoon vanilla essence |
| ¼ teaspoon salt | 2 tablespoons melted |
| 2 teaspoons baking powder | chocolate |
| ½ cup milk | ½ cup chopped nuts |

## Topping

| | |
|---|---|
| ½ cup white sugar | 2 rounded tablespoons |
| ½ cup brown sugar | cocoa |
| | 1 cup cold water |

Sift flour, sugar, salt and baking powder.
Add milk, butter, vanilla, chocolate and nuts.
Put into a pie dish.
To make the topping, mix sugar and cocoa together.
Spread over the mixture in the pan.
Pour the cold water all over and bake for 40 minutes, at
about 170°C.
Serve hot or cold.

# Bread Pudding

2 cups stale bread  
4 cups milk  
½ cup raisins (if liked)  
2 eggs, beaten until light  

½ cup sugar  
¼ teaspoon salt  
1 teaspoon vanilla  

Soak bread in milk until soft, and mash fine.  
Heat together with raisins until nearly boiling.  
Mix eggs with sugar, salt and vanilla.  
Stir into bread and milk. Pour into a baking dish.  
Set in a pan of water and bake for 1 to 1½ hours at 170°C.  
To make a spice pudding, add 1 teaspoon cinnamon,  
    ½ teaspoon cloves and ¼ teaspoon nutmeg to bread  
    while soaking.

# Cabinet Pudding

1 stale sponge cake  
currants or sultanas  

600ml hot milk  
3 eggs, beaten  

Cut up or crumble sponge cake.  
Put in a buttered pie dish.  
Sprinkle with currants or sultanas.  
Make a custard with hot milk and beaten egg. Pour this  
    over the cake.  
Leave to stand a little, then bake at 180°C for 30 minutes.  
You can use stale fruit cake if you wish.

# California Raisin Apple Cobbler

4 tart apples, peeled, cored and sliced
1 cup raisins
1 cup sugar
several knobs of butter
1 egg
1 cup flour, sifted
1 teaspoon baking powder
½ cup milk
2 tablespoons melted butter
vanilla essence to taste

Put apples in a buttered dish with raisins, ½ cup sugar and
knobs of butter.
Beat egg until very light and add the rest of the sugar.
Mix sifted flour and baking powder and add to mixture
alternately with milk.
Beat until smooth.
Add melted butter and vanilla, pour over fruit.
Bake in a moderate oven (180°C) for about 35 minutes.

# Christmas Mincemeat Meringue Pie

## Pastry

115g butter

115g sugar

1 egg

225g flour

1 teaspoon baking powder

## Topping

1 small tin crushed
   pineapple, drained

fruit mincemeat

2 egg whites

4 tablespoons sugar

glacé cherries

angelica (optional)

Cream butter and sugar. Add egg, then dry ingredients.

Roll out to fit sponge roll tin.

Prick bottom well and bake in moderate oven (180°C) for
   10 minutes.

To make the topping, mix pineapple with mincemeat and
   spread over pastry.

Cover with meringue of egg whites beaten with sugar.

Decorate with cherries and angelica.

Bake in a slow oven (120°C) until meringue is crisp and
   pastry properly cooked.

ton Chocolate Pudding, page 117

Lemon Meringue Pie, page 126

# Christmas Fruit Pie

340g short pastry
450g cooking apples, peeled and sliced
6 tablespoons chopped glacé cherries
3 large tablespoons fruit mincemeat
85g chopped almonds
2 tablespoons sherry
1 egg, beaten

Prepare short pastry and line a pie tin with half the pastry.
Mix together apples, glacé cherries, fruit mincemeat,
    almonds and sherry.
Spread on pastry, cover with remaining pastry and
    decorate edges.
Brush with egg and bake at 200°C for 40 to 45 minutes.
Serve with custard or cream.

# Handy Hint

**Silverware, to Store —**
1. Store silverware sprinkled with flour, talcum powder or powdered starch.
2. Put a small lump of camphor in the box.
3. Keep wrapped in tissue paper.
4. Never use rubber bands, as they tarnish the silver.
5. Never put pearl or ivory handled knives into hot water.

# Custard Tart

60g butter
115g flour
60g cornflour
60g sugar

½ teaspoon bicarbonate of
   soda
1 teaspoon baking powder
1 egg, well beaten

## Custard

2 breakfast cups hot milk
2 eggs, beaten
2 tablespoons sugar

Rub butter and flour, and add cornflour, sugar, bicarbonate
   of soda and baking powder.
Mix to a stiff dough with egg and roll out.
Line sandwich or oblong tins with the crust.
To make the custard, mix hot milk with eggs beaten
   with sugar.
Pour onto crust immediately before baking.
Bake in a quick oven at first (220°C), then slow
   down (180°C).
Cook on hot scone tray or shelf.
An alternative custard is made with 2 eggs, sugar to taste,
   and ½ cup cream, with nutmeg sprinkled on top.

# Devonshire Apple Curranty

4 large cooking apples
340g flour
1 small teaspoon baking
   powder
225g finely shredded suet
2 tablespoons sugar

pinch of salt
a few sultanas or currants
1 egg
a little milk
Devonshire cream to serve
   (see page 143)

Cut apples into 1–2cm cubes.
Put all ingredients except egg and milk in a basin.
Mix with the egg and a little milk, not more moist than
   a cake.
Bake at 160°C for about 1 hour.
Serve with Devonshire cream.

# Dutch Apple Tart

¼ cup butter
½ cup honey
½ teaspoon nutmeg
1 teaspoon cinnamon
2 cups flour
1 teaspoon baking powder

pinch of salt
⅓ cup butter or fat
milk
3 large cooking apples,
   peeled, cored, and sliced
cream to serve

Cream first 4 ingredients together and set aside.
Make a pastry by sifting flour, baking powder and salt.
Rub in ⅓ cup butter and mix with milk to a dough.
Line a well-greased tin about 20cm square.
Arrange apple on top of pastry and bake in a hot oven
   (220°C) for about 30 minutes.
Spread creamed mixture on top of apples.
Reduce heat and continue baking for 15 minutes.
Serve with cream.

# Golden Apple Roll

170g flour
pinch of salt
½ teaspoon baking powder
85g shredded suet

cold water to mix
apple purée, sweetened
clove or lemon essence

## Golden Sauce

¼ cup golden syrup
¾ cup boiling water

1 tablespoon butter
squeeze of lemon

Sift flour, salt and baking powder. Add suet and mix well.
Bind to a firm dough with water and roll out fairly thinly.
Spread with apple purée and essence. Leave a margin of
    pastry all round.
Roll as for jam roll and press edges firmly together.
Place in a shallow greased tin.
To make the sauce, dissolve golden syrup in boiling water.
    Add butter and lemon.
Pour sauce over roll and bake in a fairly quick oven (200°C)
    for about 40 minutes.
Baste several times.

# Gooseberry Amber

60g butter
900g gooseberries
115g caster sugar
30g cake or breadcrumbs
3 egg yolks
3 egg whites, beaten to a stiff froth
3 tablespoons caster sugar
a few drops of vanilla essence

Melt butter in a pan.
Add fruit with sugar, and let cook gently until fruit is a
    thick pulp.
Stir in crumbs and beat egg yolks well into mixture.
Slightly butter a pie dish.
Pour in mixture and put in a moderate oven (180°C). Bake
    until mixture is well set.
Mix lightly egg whites, caster sugar and vanilla.
Heap this meringue roughly all over top of the pudding and
    sprinkle a little caster sugar over.
Put into cool part of oven until meringue is pale brown.
    Serve at once.

# Gooseberry Tart

short pastry
1 cup stewed whole
  gooseberries
½ cup milk

1 teaspoon custard powder
sugar to taste
1 egg

Half cook pastry shell on a pie plate. Drain berries.
Take half a cup of the liquid, add milk, and bring to the boil.
Dissolve custard powder in the milk and stir in.
Cook and stir until smooth, adding sugar to taste.
Cool slightly then beat in egg.
Place berries in the half-cooked shell, sprinkle with sugar
    and pour over the custard.
Bake in a moderate oven (180°C) for 20 minutes.
Serve hot or cold.

# Lemon Meringue Pie

3 egg yolks, lightly beaten
½ cup honey
1 tablespoon flour
juice, flesh and grated rind
    of ½ lemon
1 teaspoon melted butter

1¼ cups milk
pie crust
3 egg whites
3 tablespoons honey
a few drops lemon juice

Mix thoroughly egg yolks, ½ cup of honey, flour, lemon
    juice, flesh and rind, and butter.
Add milk. Pour into a pie dish lined with a good crust
    pricked to prevent air bubbles.
Bake until set.
Cover with meringue made from egg whites beaten with
    honey and a few drops of lemon juice.
Bake until a nice brown.

# Lemon Pudding

½ cup sugar
1 tablespoon butter
2 tablespoons flour
pinch of salt

rind and juice of 1 lemon
1 cup milk
2 eggs, separated

Beat together the sugar and butter.
Add flour, salt, lemon rind and juice, milk and egg yolks.
Beat egg whites until thick then fold into lemon mixture.
Bake at 190°C in a buttered pie dish standing in a dish of
    hot water for about 1 hour.
Seems a strange mixture, but comes out with a crust on top,
    and like lemon cheese underneath.
Very delicious. Orange can be used instead of lemon.

# Marmalade Pudding

115g flour
160g cornflour
1 teaspoon baking powder
85g butter
2 tablespoons marmalade

1 egg
a little milk
60g sugar
115g cake crumbs
marmalade sauce to serve

Sift flour, cornflour and baking powder.
Rub in butter and add marmalade.
Add egg, milk, sugar and cake crumbs.
Bake in a greased dish in a moderate oven (180°C) for
    approximately 40 minutes.
Serve with marmalade sauce.

# Orange Hot Cake

1 cup raisins
½ cup walnuts
thinly peeled rind of 1 orange
115g butter or other shortening
2 cups sugar
1 small teaspoon baking soda
1 cup sour milk
2 eggs, beaten
pinch of salt
115g flour
115g wholemeal flour
1 small teaspoon vanilla essence
orange juice

Put raisins, walnuts and orange peel through a mincer.
    Set aside.
Cream butter and 1 cup sugar.
Dissolve baking soda in milk.
Add eggs, nut mixture, baking soda and milk, alternately
    with salt, flour, wholemeal flour and essence.
Turn into an oblong oven dish and bake in a moderate oven
    (180°C) for about 45 minutes.
While very hot, spread with remaining 1 cup sugar mixed
    with a little orange juice.
Serve hot.

Pennsylvania Pumpkin Pie, page 130

# Peach Cake

1 egg, well beaten
3 tablespoons melted butter
½ cup milk
1½ cups flour
½ cup sugar
¾ teaspoon salt
1½ teaspoons baking powder
¼ teaspoon almond essence
1 teaspoon vanilla essence
1 tin sliced peaches
3 teaspoons sugar
½ teaspoon cinnamon
cream or sauce to serve

Mix egg with butter. Add milk.
Combine flour, ½ cup sugar, salt, baking powder.
Stir in gently until batter is smooth. Add essences and stir.
Spread in a sandwich tin.
Arrange peaches on top, pressing slightly into the batter.
Sprinkle with 3 teaspoons sugar mixed with cinnamon.
Bake in a moderate oven (180°C).
Serve with cream or sauce.

# Peach Rice Pudding

peaches, peeled, stoned
and halved
chopped nuts
sprinkle of cinnamon or
nutmeg

1 cup cooked rice
½ cup sugar
2 eggs
1 large cup milk
cream to serve

Place peaches in a baking dish, cavities uppermost.
Fill cavities with nuts and spice.
Make a rice custard with remaining ingredients, and pour
over peaches.
Bake for 30 minutes.
Serve with cream.

# Pennsylvania Pumpkin Pie

2 cups cooked mashed
pumpkin
½ teaspoon nutmeg
1 teaspoon ginger
⅛ teaspoon cloves
⅛ teaspoon allspice
1 teaspoon cinnamon

½ teaspoon salt
3 egg yolks
1 cup dark brown sugar
3 cups scalded milk
3 egg whites, stiffly beaten
sweet short crust pastry

Mix pumpkin, spices, salt, egg yolks and sugar.
Add milk. Fold in egg whites.
Pour mixture into a pie dish lined with pastry brushed with
egg white.
Bake at 230°C for 15 minutes, then 180°C until baked.
For flavouring, marmalade can be added in place of spices,
and the rind and juice of 2 lemons.

# Rhubarb & Banana Betty

2 cups stale bread cut into
    small cubes
4 tablespoons butter
3 cups cut up rhubarb
1 cup brown sugar

good pinch of cinnamon
2 bananas, sliced
1 tablespoon orange juice
1 tablespoon lemon juice
2 tablespoons water

Lightly fry bread cubes in butter until light brown.
Layer rhubarb, a sprinkle of sugar and cinnamon, bananas
    and bread cubes in a buttered dish.
Repeat, finishing with bread.
Sprinkle top with two juices mixed with water.
Bake in a moderate oven (180°C) for 45 minutes.
Eat hot or cold.

# Rhubarb Sweet

450g rhubarb
water
sugar
grated rind of 1 lemon
3 egg yolks, beaten well

1 cup breadcrumbs
30g butter
sweet short crust pastry
3 egg whites
1 tablespoon sugar

Stew rhubarb with water to a pulp, sweeten and add lemon
    rind, eggs, breadcrumbs and butter.
Grease and line a pie dish with pastry, pour mixture in, and
    bake in a hot oven (220°C).
Whisk egg whites to a stiff froth with sugar.
Spread on top of pie and return to oven to set.

# Sago Cream

3 level tablespoons sago
2 level tablespoons sugar
2 cups milk

2 egg yolks, beaten
3 egg whites, stiffly beaten

Boil sago, sugar and milk in a double saucepan, stirring
    occasionally.
Add egg yolks to a little hot sago and stir. Pour back into
    cooked sago.
Pour into a buttered pie dish and stir in egg whites.
Bake in medium oven (180°C) until set, and brown.

# Strawberry Pie

short crust pastry, rolled thin
melted butter
2 cups strawberries, washed
    and hulled

½ cup sugar
2 tablespoons flour
2 teaspoons lemon juice

Line a pie dish with pastry and brush with butter.
Mix strawberries with sugar and flour. Add lemon juice.
Place in the prepared plate. Cover with pastry top. Slash for
    steam to escape.
Bake in a hot oven (220°C) for 10 minutes, then turn down
    to moderate (180°C) for 20 minutes longer.

# Spiced Prune Puff

2 cups prunes, washed
2 cups water
¾ cup sugar
a little cinnamon
a few cloves

rind of ½ lemon
½ teaspoon sugar
½ teaspoon butter
½ teaspoon cinnamon
½ teaspoon flour

## Puff Top

⅓ cup butter or dripping
½ cup sugar
1 egg, beaten
1 cup flour

½ teaspoon baking powder
1 dessertspoon cinnamon
½ cup milk

Soak prunes overnight in the water.
Stew prunes with sugar, cinnamon, cloves and lemon rind.
When tender, about 30 minutes to one hour, pour into
    a dish.
To make the puff top, cream butter and sugar, and add egg.
Sift in lightly the flour, baking powder and cinnamon.
Lastly add the milk to make a mixture that will drop from
    a spoon.
Spread puff top mixture over prunes and bake in a
    moderate oven (180°C) for 30 minutes. While pie is still
    hot, spread with a mixture of sugar, butter, cinnamon
    and flour.
Serve hot or cold.

# Sponge Crust

1 egg
1 teacup sugar (or less)
30g butter
3 tablespoons milk (or more)

1 breakfast cup flour
vanilla (if liked)
pinch of salt
hot fruit

Beat egg and sugar. Melt butter with milk and add.
Stir in flour, vanilla and salt. Pour over hot fruit.
Cook in a hot oven (220°C) for about 20 minutes.

# Tenterden Apple Pie

1.35kg cooking apples
115g sugar
cloves
½ teacup water
115g cheese, cut into thin
    slices

pepper
nutmeg
½ teaspoon caster sugar
short pastry, rolled out

Peel, core and cut apples into thick slices.
Place a layer of apples in a pie dish. Sprinkle with 1
    tablespoon sugar.
Add another layer of apples and sugar, and the cloves.
Pour in the water.
Cover the apples with cheese.
Sprinkle with the merest suggestion of pepper, a little
    nutmeg and the caster sugar.
Line edge of the pie dish with pastry and put on
    pastry cover.
Press edges together and raise them slightly with a knife.
Sprinkle with caster sugar and bake in a good oven (180°C)
    for 40 to 50 minutes.

# Toffee Apple Pudding

225g flour
140g shredded suet
1 teaspoon baking powder
pinch of salt
water to mix
apples, cored, peeled, sliced and cooked
6 teaspoons brown sugar

## Toffee

60g butter
60g brown sugar

Mix flour, suet, baking powder, salt and water, and
    roll out thin.
Carefully cover sides of a pie dish with toffee.
Line the dish with half the suet crust.
Pile in plenty of apples.
Sprinkle with brown sugar.
Cover with remaining crust.
Bake in a hot oven (220°C) for 1¼ hours, or until done.
This pudding may be served from the pie dish. Or turn out
    onto a separate dish and the rich toffee sauce will be
    seen to cover it.

# Yorkshire Goathland Treacle Tart

short pastry
1 breakfast cup dry
   breadcrumbs
1 breakfast cup mixed fruit
   (sultanas, currant and
   peel)
1 apple, peeled, cored and
   grated

juice and grated rind of
   1 lemon
1 salt spoon spice
1 salt spoon ground ginger
2 tablespoons treacle
1 tablespoon sugar
2 tablespoons milk
brown sugar for sprinkling

Line a pie dish with pastry.

Mix all other ingredients (except milk and brown sugar)
   together and put over pastry.

Cover with top layer of pastry.

Brush over top with milk, sprinkle with brown sugar.

Bake at 180°C for about 40 minutes.

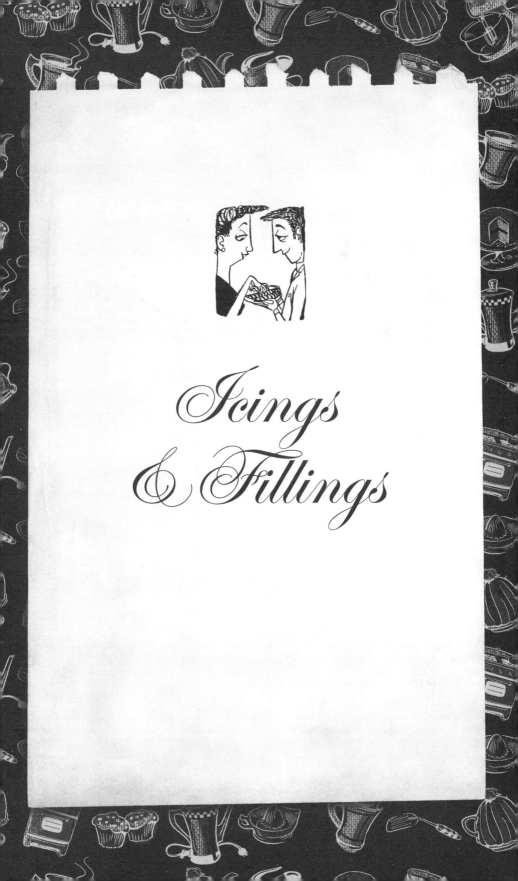

# Icings
# & Fillings

# Almond Icing - Plain

450g icing sugar
225g caster sugar
115g ground almonds

whole eggs or yolks to bind
almond essence

Sieve icing sugar, add caster sugar and ground almonds.
Rub all well together, bind to a nice consistency with
the eggs.
Add essence and knead all together.
Roll out, use as desired.
The more ground almonds used, the longer the icing will
keep soft.

# Almond Paste - For Christmas Cake

225g ground almonds
450g icing sugar

1 whole egg, beaten
white of ½ an extra egg

Mix almonds and sugar well together.
Add beaten egg and about half the white of another.
Mix over a low heat until a stiff paste but it must be only
warm.
Dredge a board with icing sugar and roll paste to required
shape and thickness.
Brush top of cake with egg white to make paste stick, and
press paste onto cake.

# Apple Filling

4 large apples
juice of 1 orange
a little grated orange peel
½ cup brown sugar

2 tablespoons melted butter
 or cream
2 tablespoons honey
pinch of cinnamon (optional)

Bake apples.
Mix apple pulp with other ingredients.
Beat, and keep in little jars.
A pinch of cinnamon may also be added.

# Apple Lemon Curd

225g apples, peeled, cored
 and cut up
juice and rind of 1½ lemons

2 eggs, beaten
1 cup caster sugar
60g butter

Cook apples until soft. Beat to a pulp.
Add lemon juice and rind.
Add eggs with sugar to mixture, and beat well.
Melt butter in a basin and add the mixture to it.
Cook over a double boiler and stir until mixture is thick,
    about 20 minutes.
Put in jars, and cover tightly when cool.

# Banana Butter

4 bananas
225g sugar
2 eggs

juice of 2 lemons
grated rind of 1 lemon
2 tablespoons butter

Mash bananas, and beat in sugar and eggs.
Put into a saucepan with other ingredients and cook until
like lemon honey with banana flavour.

# Banana Butter Frosting

1 large banana mashed
smooth
1½ teaspoons lemon juice

¼ cup butter or margarine
3½ cups sifted icing sugar

Mix banana and lemon juice.
Beat butter until creamy.
Add sugar and banana alternately.
Keep beating until frosting is light and fluffy.

# Boston Mocha Frosting

¼ cup sweetened
condensed milk
1½ tablespoons strong
black coffee

1 teaspoon vanilla essence
2¼ cups icing sugar
2 teaspoons cocoa
⅛ teaspoon salt

Blend condensed milk, coffee and vanilla.
Sift sugar, cocoa and salt, and add.
Blend and spread.

# Butter Frosting

2 tablespoons butter
¼ cup sweetened condensed milk
1½ cups finely sifted icing sugar
½ teaspoon vanilla (or other essence)

Cream butter and condensed milk thoroughly.
Gradually add icing sugar. Add essence.
Beat until frosting is smooth, creamy and light in colour.


# Chocolate Foam

1 teaspoon gelatine dissolved in ½ cup hot cocoa
a little vanilla essence
1 egg white, beaten
1 cup sifted icing sugar

Let cocoa and gelatine cool. Add vanilla.
Beat egg white and gradually add cocoa mixture.
Gradually stir in icing sugar.
Spread on cake or use as filling.

# Coconut Orange Filling

½ cup sugar
4 tablespoons flour
dash of salt
⅓ cup orange juice
3 tablespoons lemon juice
2 tablespoons water

1 egg, well beaten
2 tablespoons butter
1½ teaspoons grated orange
    rind
¼ cup desiccated coconut

Combine sugar, flour and salt on top of a double boiler.
Add juices, water and egg.
Cook over rapidly boiling water for 10 minutes,
    stirring constantly.
Remove from heat and add butter and orange rind. Beat.
    Fold in coconut.
Makes a filling to spread generously between two
    23cm layers.


# Date Filling

115g dates
1 tablespoon sugar
2 tablespoons water

juice of ½ lemon
grated rind of 1 lemon

Boil dates, sugar and water until soft.
Add lemon juice and rind.
Beat well.

# Devonshire Cream

Set a shallow pan full of fresh whole milk in a cool place for
   12 to 24 hours.
Carefully carry pan to stove and bring slowly to scalding
   point — until the thick, yellow cream begins to wrinkle.
Put back in cool place until quite cold. Skim carefully with
   a perforated skimmer.
The cream should come off in a thick blanket.

# English Lemon Filling

| | |
|---|---|
| 3 tablespoons butter | 2 eggs, beaten until thick |
| juice of 2 lemons | 1 cup white sugar |
| grated rind of ½ lemon | pinch of salt |

Put butter in top of double boiler.
Add lemon juice and rind.
Stir eggs into sugar.
Add salt and stir all into first mixture.
Cook and stir over hot water until thick. Cool.
May be used as a cake, tart or sweet sandwich filling.

# Everyday Filling

| | |
|---|---|
| 2 tablespoons butter | essence of choice |
| 4 tablespoons sugar | 2 tablespoons boiling water |

Put butter, sugar and essence in a basin. Add boiling water.
Beat thoroughly until like whipped cream.
Leave for 15 minutes, then use.

# Filling with Condensed Milk

Cream together equal quantities of butter and sweetened
condensed milk.
Add either minced dates, sultanas or preserved ginger, or
cherries, or a mixture.

# Fluffy Coffee Icing

| | |
|---|---|
| 4 tablespoons butter | ¼ teaspoon cinnamon |
| 1 egg white, unbeaten | 3 tablespoons strong cold |
| about 2½ cups icing sugar | coffee |

Cream the butter.
Add unbeaten egg white and 1 cup of the sugar.
Stir in cinnamon. Add remainder of sugar alternately with
cold coffee.
Icing should have a fluffy texture, and be spread on cake
roughly.

# Fluffy Mocha Frosting

| | |
|---|---|
| 1 tablespoon butter | ¼ teaspoon salt |
| 2 cups sifted icing sugar | ½ teaspoon vanilla essence |
| 1 tablespoon cocoa | 2 tablespoons strong coffee |

Beat butter to cream. Add all other ingredients and beat
until smooth. Spread between layers of gingerbread,
or on top.

# Gingerbread Filling

1 cup sweetened
  condensed milk
3 tablespoons lemon juice

6 tablespoons mashed
  cheese (use silver fork)
gingerbread

Mix condensed milk with lemon juice, and stir until thick.
Add cheese. Beat until smooth.
Spread between layers of gingerbread, or on top.

# Grapefruit Cheese

115g butter
2 cups sugar
juice of 3 large grapefruit

grated rind of 1 grapefruit
2 eggs, well beaten

Put butter, sugar, and grapefruit juice and rind into a large
  basin or double saucepan.
Stand over pan of boiling water.
When melted and blended together, add eggs, stirring
  constantly and thoroughly until mixture thickens.
Pour into small pots, and cover when cold.
This will keep a considerable time, and is a delightful
  change from lemon.

# Icing for Lamingtons

60g butter
3 teaspoons cocoa
½ teaspoon vanilla

4 tablespoons water
1 cup icing sugar
coconut

Put all ingredients (except coconut) in a pan and stir until
blended. Do not boil.
Let cool, then dip in pieces of sponge (or stale Madeira
cake). Roll in coconut.

# Lemon Cheese

85g butter
225g sugar
4 wine biscuits, finely
crushed

juice and grated rind of
3 lemons
4 eggs, well beaten

Melt together first 4 ingredients. Add eggs.
Cook until mixture thickens, stirring all the time. Do not
boil or it will spoil!

# Lemon Cheese ~ For Tartlets

1 cup sugar
juice and grated rind of
4 lemons

2 tablespoons butter
2 eggs

Cook until thick in a double boiler.

# Lemon Cheese ~ Good

4 eggs, beaten just a little
juice and grated rind of
4 lemons

225g butter
450g sugar

Cook in a double boiler, or a basin in a saucepan of
boiling water.
See that water boils all the time.
Keep in airtight jars.

# Lemon Cheese ~ Without Butter

1 cup water
4 tablespoons sugar
juice of 2 large lemons

1 heaped tablespoon
cornflour
1 egg, well beaten
a little milk (if needed)

Boil together water, sugar and lemon juice.
Mix cornflour with egg, and milk if necessary.
Pour boiling liquid over it.
Mix and return to pan.
Boil for 5 minutes.

# Lemon Honey – Without Eggs

60g butter
1 breakfast cup sugar
juice and grated rind of
    2 large lemons

1 tablespoon cornflour
    moistened with water

Melt butter and sugar very slowly with lemon juice
    and rind.
When sugar is dissolved, add cornflour.
Remove from heat while stirring in cornflour.
Cook all very slowly until clear golden.

# Simple Marshmallow

2 dessertspoons gelatine
    soaked in 1 cup water
1 breakfast cup sugar
a few drops of vanilla or
    other essence

shortbread (or other biscuit)
icing
nuts as topping

Mix gelatine with sugar and boil in a saucepan for
    10 minutes.
Add essence. Let cool.
Beat until white and thick.
Spread on shortbread, etc.
Ice when cold and sprinkle with nuts.

# Marshmallow Filling

30g powdered gelatine
2 cups water
450g sugar
pinch of salt

1 teaspoon vanilla essence
biscuits
nuts and cherries to
decorate

Put gelatine in 1 cup water and stand for 10 minutes.
Add other cup of water. Put on stove to melt.
When melted, add sugar, salt and vanilla, and boil gently
    for 30 minutes.
Cool in a basin then beat until like a snowball.
Almost cover biscuits and decorate with chopped nuts
    and cherries.

# Meringue Cake Topping

1 egg white
1 tablespoon sugar

Beat egg white and sugar to a meringue.
Spread about 3mm thick over top of cake mixture
    before cooking.

# Mocha Icing & Filling

1½ tablespoons butter
2½ cups sugar
2½ tablespoons cocoa

4 tablespoons strong coffee
¼ teaspoon salt

Cream butter and sugar.
Add cocoa, coffee and salt. Stir until smooth.
Spread between layers and on top of cake.


# Mock Almond Icing

equal amounts icing sugar
   and ground rice
1 egg

about 2 teaspoons almond
   essence
a little lemon juice

Sift icing sugar, mix well with ground rice.
Add egg, essence and lemon juice.
Work well together.
If well blended, this closely resembles real almond icing.


# Mock Almond Paste

3 egg yolks, beaten
900g icing sugar
225g desiccated coconut

2 teaspoons almond
   essence

Mix egg yolks with dry ingredients.
Beat in the essence.
Stand in a basin in a saucepan of boiling water.
Knead well for a few minutes.
If too dry, add a little water.

# Mock Cream (1)

2 heaped tablespoons full
    cream milk powder
2 teaspoons sugar

½ cup fresh milk (or more if
    cream is required thinner)
essence of choice

Mix milk powder with sugar.

Stir in fresh milk.

Add essence and beat with an egg beater for a minute
    or two.

This can be used as a topping for trifle, or if made thinner,
    as a pudding sauce.


# Mock Cream (2)

2 cups milk
2 tablespoons full cream
    milk powder
2 teaspoons gelatine
    dissolved in 1 dessert-
    spoon boiling water

1 teaspoon sugar
a little vanilla essence

Warm milk to blood heat.

Mix milk powder to a paste with a little milk, then stir in
    the rest.

Add gelatine and sugar.

Stand aside to chill thoroughly, to let the gelatine set a little.
    Then beat again.

# Mock Cream (3)

2 level tablespoons cornflour
1 cup milk
30g butter

15g sugar
essence if desired

Mix cornflour with a little milk.
Warm the remaining milk in a saucepan.
Add cornflour and return to pan.
Stir over heat until well cooked. Put aside to cool.
Cream butter and sugar very well.
Beat in thickened cornflour and essence, by the teaspoonful.
Continue to beat until creamy.
The above quantity makes about ½ cup of cream, very
     similar to whipped cream.

# Mock Whipped Cream

1 teaspoon gelatine mixed
   with 3 tablespoons
   boiling water
115g butter

pinch of salt
1½ tablespoons sugar
vanilla or lemon essence
½ teaspoon cream of tartar

Stir gelatine in the boiling water until dissolved.
Put butter, sugar, salt and essence into a basin.
     Cream a little.
Add cream of tartar. Add dissolved gelatine.
Whip well (about 10 minutes) until it looks like
     whipped cream.
An excellent filling for sponge or puffs.

# Orange Filling

85g flour
1 cup sugar
grated rind of 1 orange
½ cup orange juice

3 tablespoons lemon juice
¼ cup water
1 egg, slightly beaten
1 dessertspoon butter

Combine ingredients in the order given.
Cook in a double boiler for 10 minutes, stirring
constantly. Cool.
May also be used as a filling for éclairs, or with shredded
coconut for pastry tarts.

# Orange Filling for Sponge

1 tablespoon gelatine
juice of 1 large orange
1 cup cream

a little sugar
1 teaspoon brandy
grated rind of 1 orange

Soak gelatine in orange juice.
Whip cream with a little sugar and brandy.
Add orange rind.
Stand gelatine and juice in a cup in a saucepan of
boiling water.
Stir until gelatine is dissolved. Let cool.
Add to cream, and whip again.

# Passionfruit Honey

10 passionfruit
1 tablespoon butter

1 cup sugar
1 egg, beaten

Heat all in a saucepan over boiling water until thick,
    stirring with a wooden spoon.
A delicious filling.

# Pineapple Filling – Quick

1 cup icing sugar
1 tablespoon pineapple juice

2 egg whites, whipped stiff
finely chopped pineapple

Beat icing sugar and pineapple juice into egg whites.
Stir in as much chopped pineapple as the icing will hold.
Add a little more sugar if necessary.

# Plain White Icing

2 tablespoons hot milk
1 teaspoon essence (orange, pineapple or other)
about 1⅓ cups icing sugar

Put hot milk in a small bowl. Add essence.
Cream in sugar until the right consistency.

# White Icing – Ordinary Sugar

1 breakfast cup plain
white sugar
15g fresh butter

½ breakfast cup milk
essence (of choice)

Put sugar in a saucepan. Add butter and milk.
Boil for 8 minutes, stirring well.
Flavour with essence and beat until thick as cream.
Spread over cake with a knife and it will be white when cold.
Double this quantity for a large cake.

# *Index*